New Searchlight Series

Under the general editorship of
George W. Hoffman and G. Etzel Pearcy

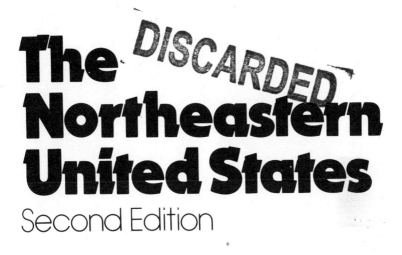

The Northeastern United States

Second Edition

Lewis M. Alexander
University of Rhode Island

D. VAN NOSTRAND COMPANY
New York · Cincinnati · Toronto · London · Melbourne

D. Van Nostrand Company Regional Offices:
New York   Cincinnati   Millbrae

D. Van Nostrand Company International Offices:
London   Toronto   Melbourne

Library of Congress Catalog Card Number: 75-41660
ISBN: 0-442-29749-1

Published by D. Van Nostrand Company
450 West 33rd Street, New York, N. Y.   10001

10 9 8 7 6 5 4 3 2 1

Preface

The Northeast is a region of contrasts. On the one hand, there are the gleaming skyscrapers of New York, Boston, Philadelphia, and Baltimore; on the other, the slums of Harlem, the South Bronx, Roxbury, and South Philadelphia, where tens of thousands of people live in conditions that are well below the poverty level. The summer beaches of Cape Cod and Long Island and the vacation retreats of the Maine coast are in sharp contrast with the former textile towns of southeastern Massachusetts and Rhode Island or the coal towns of western Pennsylvania.

It is a region rich in tradition, a tradition reflected in its battlefields, whaling museums, covered bridges, and other monuments to the nation's historic past. Even the cities, such as Boston, New York, and Philadelphia, retain elements of the past—in their narrow streets, row houses, and parks dating back to colonial times. The Northeast was the focus of America's early development—both as a colony and as an independent nation—and the vestiges of this past are everywhere to be seen.

The forces of change are also apparent in the Northeast—in the nuclear power stations, the jet airports, the electronics plants, and the population sprawl that is gradually turning parts of the area into great urban agglomerations. Change is reflected in the movement of people away from once prosperous rural areas, in the flight of the middle-income groups from the central cities to the suburbs, and in the migration of low-income families into the downtown areas of the cities. The expanding network of superhighways, the urban-renewal programs, the new recreation areas—these too represent changes in the way of life of the people of the Northeast and in the landscape of the region that they occupy.

Urbanization and *technology* are the two keys to present-day developments in the northeastern United States—urbanization bringing millions of people into the satellite cities and towns surrounding the major metropolises, and technology developing new communications systems, new industries, and new wealth for the area. But can technology provide answers to the basic problems brought about by urbanization—the problems of rehabilitation of slums; adequate transportation for cities; and relief for depressed rural areas, from which population and wealth have fled? Can it halt the decline of such industries as textiles, coal mining, and shoe manufacturing? Can it rationalize farming, so that the Northeast can compete successfully with other parts of the nation?

This book seeks to treat these and similar questions through a regional survey of the Northeast in the mid-1970s. It analyzes the forces of tradition and change against the background of the Northeast's physical environment and historical development. The problems of economic, social, and political adjustment are considered in terms of the various geographical subregions of the area, with the aim of shedding new light on the impact these changes have had on the landscape and people of the Northeastern United States.

Lewis M. Alexander

Contents

Maps

Tables

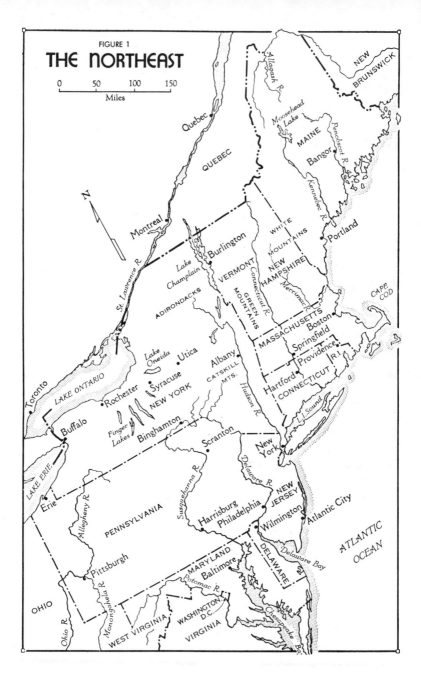

FIGURE 1

THE NORTHEAST

0   50   100   150
Miles

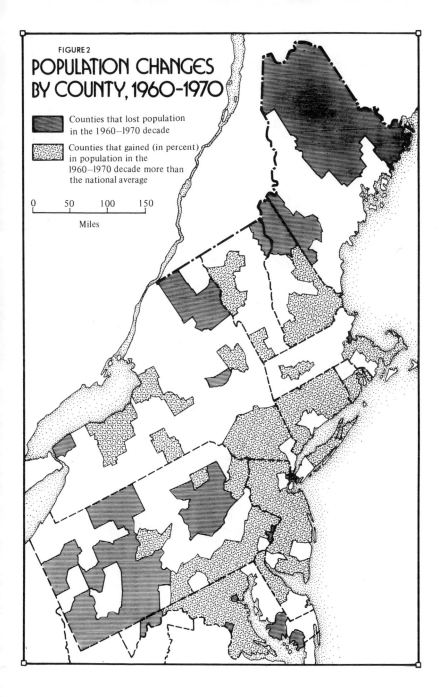

FIGURE 2

POPULATION CHANGES
BY COUNTY, 1960-1970

Counties that lost population
in the 1960–1970 decade

Counties that gained (in percent)
in population in the
1960–1970 decade more than
the national average

0   50   100   150

Miles

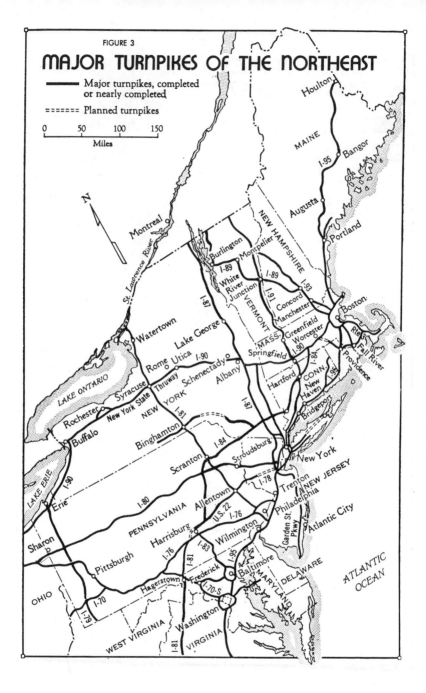

FIGURE 3

MAJOR TURNPIKES OF THE NORTHEAST

—— Major turnpikes, completed or nearly completed

===== Planned turnpikes

0   50   100   150
Miles

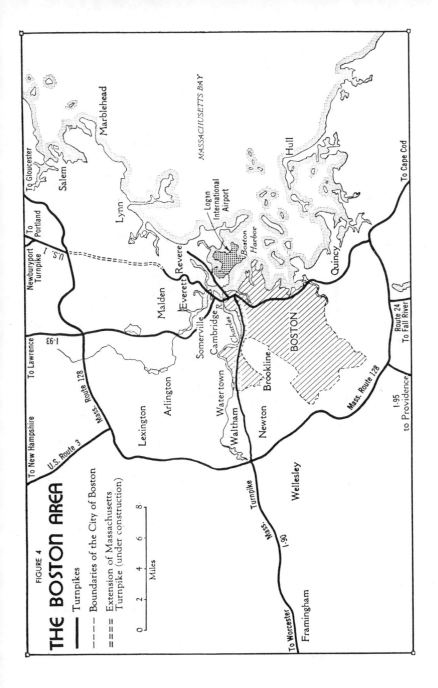

FIGURE 4

THE BOSTON AREA

━━━ Turnpikes

- - - - Boundaries of the City of Boston

==== Extension of Massachusetts Turnpike (under construction)

Miles
0 2 4 6 8

To Worcester
Framingham

Mass. Turnpike
I-90

Wellesley

U.S. Route 3
To New Hampshire

Mass. Route 128

Lexington

Arlington

Waltham

Watertown

Newton

Brookline

Mass. Route 128

I-95
to Providence

Route 24
To Fall River

To Lawrence

I-93

Somerville

Cambridge

Charles R.

BOSTON

Quincy

To Cape Cod

Newburyport
Turnpike

To Portland

U.S. 1

Malden

Everett

Revere

Logan
International
Airport

Boston
Harbor

To Gloucester

Salem

Marblehead

Lynn

Hull

MASSACHUSETTS BAY

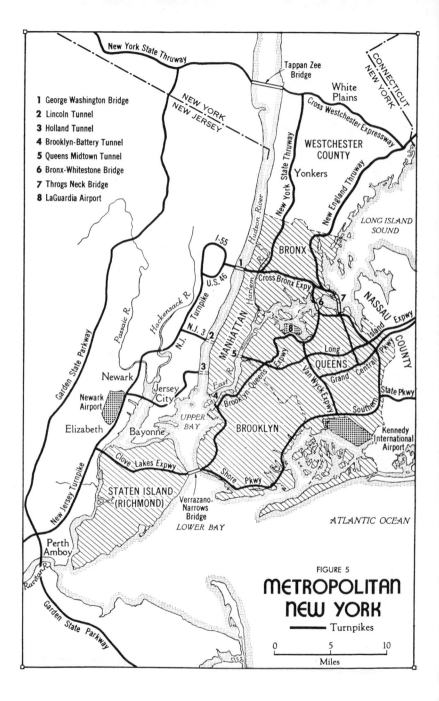

1 George Washington Bridge
2 Lincoln Tunnel
3 Holland Tunnel
4 Brooklyn-Battery Tunnel
5 Queens Midtown Tunnel
6 Bronx-Whitestone Bridge
7 Throgs Neck Bridge
8 LaGuardia Airport

New York State Thruway

Tappan Zee Bridge

CONNECTICUT
NEW YORK

White Plains

Cross Westchester Expressway

NEW YORK
NEW JERSEY

WESTCHESTER COUNTY

Yonkers

New York State Thruway

New England Thruway

LONG ISLAND SOUND

I-55

BRONX

U.S. 46

Hudson River

Cross Bronx Expy

Harlem R.

NASSAU COUNTY

Passaic R.

Hackensack R.

N.J. Turnpike

N.J. 3

MANHATTAN

6

7

8

Island Expwy

Garden State Parkway

Newark

Newark Airport

Jersey City

East R.

Long Island Expwy

QUEENS

Grand Central

State Pkwy

Elizabeth

Bayonne

UPPER BAY

Brooklyn-Queens Expwy

Van Wyck Expwy

Southern

Kennedy International Airport

BROOKLYN

Clove Lakes Expwy

Shore Pkwy

New Jersey Turnpike

STATEN ISLAND (RICHMOND)

Verrazano-Narrows Bridge

LOWER BAY

ATLANTIC OCEAN

Perth Amboy

Raritan R.

Garden State Parkway

FIGURE 5

METROPOLITAN NEW YORK

━━━ Turnpikes

0   5   10

Miles

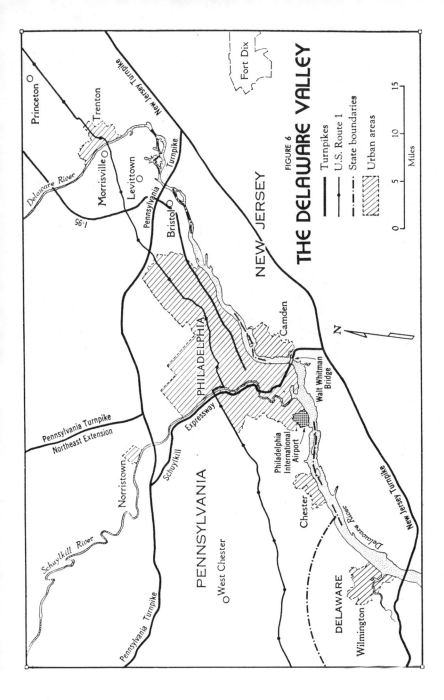

FIGURE 6

THE DELAWARE VALLEY

Turnpikes
U.S. Route 1
State boundaries
Urban areas

0   5   10   15
Miles

N

Princeton

Trenton

New Jersey Turnpike

Morrisville

Levittown

Delaware River

Pennsylvania Turnpike

I-95

Bristol

Fort Dix

NEW JERSEY

Camden

Walt Whitman Bridge

Pennsylvania Turnpike
Northeast Extension

Norristown

Schuylkill

Schuylkill River

PENNSYLVANIA

West Chester

Expressway

PHILADELPHIA

Philadelphia International Airport

Chester

Delaware River

New Jersey Turnpike

Pennsylvania Turnpike

DELAWARE

Wilmington

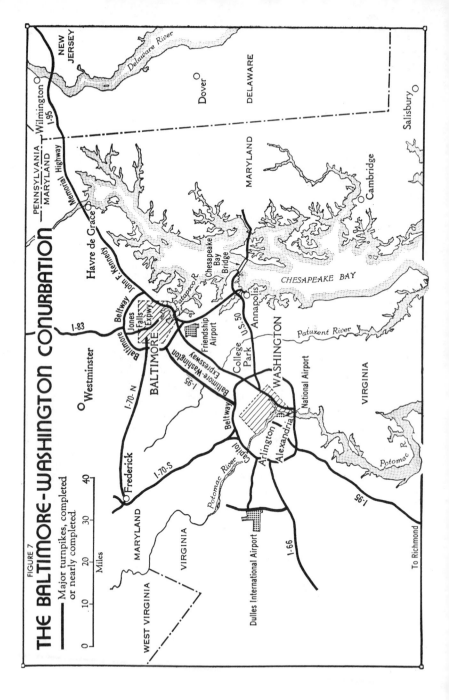

FIGURE 7

THE BALTIMORE-WASHINGTON CONURBATION

Major turnpikes, completed
or nearly completed.

Miles
0   10   20   30   40

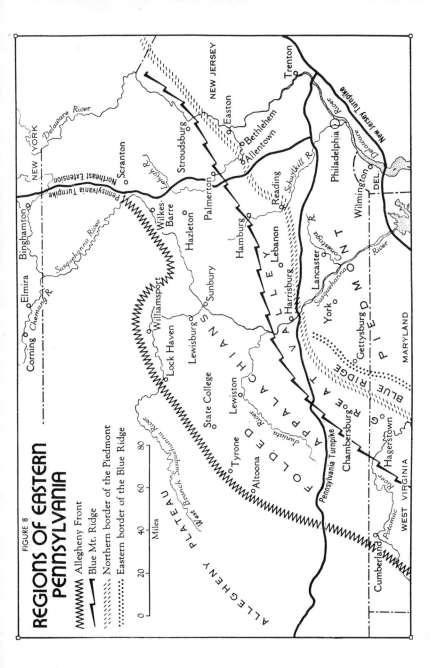

FIGURE 8

REGIONS OF EASTERN PENNSYLVANIA

MWMWM Allegheny Front
⌐⌐⌐⌐⌐   Blue Mt. Ridge
,,,,,,,, Northern border of the Piedmont
:::::::: Eastern border of the Blue Ridge

Miles
0   20   40   60   80

1 The Land and Its People

The physical environment is a basic component in any analysis of a geographic region. The environment offers certain opportunities for development as well as limitations in choice, such as extreme cold, aridity, or steep slope. The opportunities and limitations in any particular locale vary in significance with the passing of time. The harbors along the Maine coast, for example, were once important for commercial shipping; now they are summer recreation attractions. The colonial farmhouses of western Connecticut have become weekend retreats for New Yorkers, while the seemingly endless ridges of central Pennsylvania, which once forced traffic to detour many miles, have now been pierced by turnpike tunnels. Scranton's hard coal, Rutland's marble, and Nantucket's whale oil—these and other resources have been rendered partially or wholly obsolete by changing technology. This same technology may, of course, bring radical changes to the physical environment itself—through deforestation, soil erosion, air pollution, strip mining, or the damming of rivers. The interplay between man and his physical milieu also includes the factors of population size in any given area and the patterns of settlement. Traditional settlement patterns and ways of life will in time give way to changing conditions of the physical environment, although aspects of the former way of life remain as features of the

1

landscape. In this chapter we shall consider the physical landscape of the Northeast[1] and the settlement patterns of the people who inhabit the area in terms of the interaction of tradition and change.

LANDFORMS

The landforms of the Northeast—that is, its plains, hills, and mountains—had extremely important effects on the early history of settlement patterns, on routes of transit between the eastern seaboard and the interior, and on the sites of communities along the coast toward the sea. Somewhat later, the fertile valleys of Pennsylvania and the waterpower sites of New England and New York lured settlers away from the seaboard. Although such factors as these are far less important today in influencing settlement patterns, their mark is still visible. It shows itself in the distribution of the older cities and towns and in the vestiges of bygone farms and factories, which still exist throughout much of this area.

The Northeast may be subdivided physiographically into two major regions, the *coastal lowlands* and the *interior highlands.* Both of these regions trend generally northeast-southwest and contain within themselves various subregions. The coastal lowlands begin in the north with Cape Cod and Long Island. South of New York City the lowlands broaden; their western boundary is the fall line, a line of rapids marking the head of navigation of rivers flowing down to the sea. This line, starting to the west of New York, extends southwest through Trenton, Philadelphia, Wilmington, Baltimore, and Washington. Not only does it mark the limits of navigation—and is thus a logical point for the location of port cities—but it also previously represented sites for waterpower development in the early era

1. The Northeast is taken here as including the six New England states, New York, New Jersey, Pennsylvania, Delaware, Maryland, and the District of Columbia. Such a region has a number of unifying elements binding it together, but there are no abrupt transitions encountered in crossing the southern and southwestern boundaries of the Northeast into neighboring Virginia, West Virginia, and Ohio.

of industrialization. East of the fall line, the coastal plain extends across parts of New Jersey, Delaware, and Maryland, with predominantly sandy soils and level or gently rolling terrain, rising to less than 500 feet in elevation. The Atlantic shoreline is sandy, with many spits, bars, and lagoons. Cape Cod, with its nearly 400 miles of beaches, is a prime summer vacation area. To the south of the Cape are the islands of Nantucket and Martha's Vineyard; to the southwest are Block Island and the two eastern peninsulas of Long Island. Along the south shore of Long Island, and from Sandy Hook south in New Jersey, Delaware, and Maryland, are a series of offshore bars on which are located such vacation spots as Asbury Park, Atlantic City, and Rehoboth Beach.

Many rivers originate in the interior highlands and flow across the coastal plains to the sea; among them the Hudson, the Delaware, and the Susquehanna. These afford natural routes into the interior. The Hudson, for example, has a broad valley and connections via the Mohawk Corridor with the Great Lakes, and through the Champlain Lowland with the St. Lawrence. Embayment of the coastline has produced the Chesapeake and Delaware bays, New York Harbor, Narragansett Bay in Rhode Island, and Boston Harbor. Thus, the coastal plain provides access both to the sea and to the interior sections of the Northeast. At various times in its history, the Northeast has been oriented predominantly seaward; while at other times, it has tended to look inward toward the development of the continent's resources.

North and west of the coastal plain are the various highland areas: the *New England Uplands*, the *Adirondacks*, and the *Appalachian Highlands*. The Appalachian Highlands contain four subsections—the Catskills, the Allegheny Plateau, the Folded Appalachians, and the Piedmont. Associated with these highland areas are the Hudson-Champlain Lowlands, the Mohawk Valley, the Ontario Plain, and the Great Valley of Pennsylvania and Maryland. Each of these regions has its own distinct landscape. Over the years the inhabitants have made varied adjustments to their physical environments.

The New England Uplands are composed of ancient crystalline rocks that have been folded by slow geological processes into a complex of hills and low mountains. Above the general level of the Uplands are the White Mountains of New Hampshire, a granite mass rising to over 6,000 feet, the lower Green Mountains of Vermont, and the Taconics and Berkshires of western Massachusetts and Connecticut, which rise to over 3,000 feet. Because the New England Uplands were subjected to glaciation, the drainage is one of swift-flowing rivers and numerous lakes and marshes. Soils are often thin or filled with glacial boulders, which the original farmers were forced to dig out before cultivation was possible. Many of the rivers and lakes still provide excellent fishing for sportsmen.

From the Boston Basin northward, the coastline is one of rocky headlands, inlets, and offshore islands. Rivers such as the Penobscot, the Kennebec, and the Merrimack all flow to the sea and afford both waterpower potential and a means for transporting logs downstream to the sawmills. Stretching along the coast are once-busy harbors, such as Ellsworth, Camden, and York, which were once noted both for fishing and for their merchant fleets. Present-day ports include Portsmouth, Portland, and Gloucester; these, too, have lost much of their former importance. Here, also, are such tourist centers as Bar Harbor, Ogunquit, and Newburyport, which were among the most fashionable of the summer resorts in the nation some decades ago. South of Boston, rivers such as the Taunton, Blackstone, and Housatonic were once important for power but are now little used. The Connecticut River, flowing south through Massachusetts and Connecticut in a broad valley, is the one mature river east of the Hudson.

The New England Uplands extend a few miles into New York State to the Hudson-Champlain Lowland. One prong of the Uplands stretches down to Manhattan Island, where the resistant rocks form the foundation for New York's skyscrapers. Another prong crosses the Hudson River at West Point, extending on into New Jersey. The Hudson-Champlain Lowland above West Point is a broad, structural valley, separating the New England Uplands to the east from the Adirondacks and the Appalachian Highlands to the west. It provides easy access to Canada, as evidenced by its wealth of Revolutionary War battlegrounds, such as Bennington and Saratoga. Lake Champlain, a long, narrow body of water that extends into Canada, occupies the northern part of the Lowland. East of the lake, between it and the Green Mountains, is a narrow, fertile area of low hills in Vermont and New York State where dairying is an important activity. The Hudson River enters the Lowlands from the Adirondacks, close to the southern end of Lake Champlain. At Albany it receives the Mohawk River, coming from the west through the Mohawk Valley. This valley, separating the Adirondacks from the Appalachian Highlands to the south, forms a natural lowland route to the Great Lakes and beyond them to the Midwest. Through this depression runs the Erie Canal, connecting New York with the West. South of Lake Ontario, the Mohawk Valley broadens into an extensive lowland area—the so-called Ontario Plain of western New York State.

The Adirondacks are a granitic mass, heavily forested and rising to over 5,000 feet in elevation. There are numerous lakes here, and the area is an important recreation center. South of the Mohawk Valley are the Catskill Mountains, which are part of the Appalachian Highlands. These mountains are a sandstone mass rising to over 4,000 feet. Like the Adirondacks, they are a forested, lake-studded area, which has never been intensively settled. Because of their proximity to New York City, they have a well-developed, year-round recreation industry.

The Appalachian Highlands cover southern New York State, western New Jersey, and all of Pennsylvania, as well as western Maryland. West of the Catskills, in southern New York State and Pennsylvania, the Highlands have been deeply dissected by such rivers as the Delaware, the Susquehanna, the Allegheny, the Monongahela, and the Ohio in western Pennsylvania. In the northern, glaciated part of the Highlands, the relief is gentler and the valleys are broader than in the nonglaciated sector. In New York State, glacial action resulted in the formation of the long, narrow Finger Lakes, of which Cayuga and Seneca are perhaps the best known.

The general level of the Highlands rises from less than 2,000 feet in New York and northeastern Pennsylvania to over 3,000 feet in western Pennsylvania. A north-south escarpment in central Pennsylvania marks the eastern rim of the Allegheny Plateau, which is an extremely rugged area rich with resources of bituminous coal. Just west of Altoona, the Penn-Central Railroad ascends the escarpment by its famous Horseshoe Curve. The Plateau extends across western Pennsylvania into West Virginia and easternmost Ohio.

In Pennsylvania, east of the Allegheny Plateau, are the Folded Appalachians, a region of long parallel hills and longitudinal valleys. Stretching northeast from Cumberland, Maryland to the Scranton-Wilkes-Barre sector is an area important for its anthracite coal resources—particularly around Scranton and Wilkes-Barre. In the eastern part of the Folded Appalachians is the long, gently rolling Great Valley, with its excellent limestone soils. It trends southwest across Pennsylvania and Maryland, ultimately linking with the Shenandoah Valley of Virginia. In northern Pennsylvania it is known as the Lehigh Valley; farther south, as the Lebanon Valley; and in Maryland, as the Cumberland Valley. By the mid-eighteenth century, settlers from the eastern seaboard—particularly the Pennsylvania Dutch—had begun farming the fertile land. The eastern border of the Great Valley is marked by a pronounced ridge, through which the Delaware, Lehigh, Schuylkill, and Susquehanna rivers have cut in dramatic gaps. A rolling, fertile upland area—the Piedmont—lies between this ridge and the coastal plain. It contains broad valleys, including the red-soiled Triassic area of New Jersey (west of New York City) and the valleys of Lancaster and York in Pennsylvania.

The landforms of the Northeast possess neither the grandeur of those in the West nor the unbroken sameness of parts of the Middle West. The region lacks a uniting river system such as the Mississippi and in many places, steep slopes, thin soils, or coastal marshes precluded early settlement. But in time some of the marshes were filled in and built upon, steep slopes were utilized for recreation or forestry, and with changing technology, the people of the Northeast learned to utilize those elements of the land that they found to be useful. Today, *location*, with respect to cities, transportation routes, or the sea, is frequently more important in determining settlement and land use than is the nature of the landforms themselves.

CLIMATE

The climate of the Northeast can be classified as humid mid-latitude, with cold winters, warm summers, and distinct fall and spring seasons. This climate was conducive to settlement by the European colonists; although they were forced to protect themselves against the long, cold winters that are characteristic of most of the region, and the occasional summer droughts, hurricanes, and tornadoes. The climate of the Northeast was not unlike the one that the Europeans had known before they came to the New World, and thus the early settlers were accustomed to it.

Average monthly temperatures of Northeastern winters range from 34°F. in Washington, D.C. to 9°F. in Aroostook County, Maine, and 12°F. in northern New Hampshire. Average summer temperatures vary from about 65°F. in northern New England to 75°F. in Delaware and Maryland. Annual precipitation is generally 40–45 inches and is distributed fairly evenly throughout the year. Nowhere is precipitation inadequate, in normal years, for agriculture. Northern New England and parts of western Pennsylvania have a heavy snowfall in winter. Similarly, from Buffalo eastward through Syracuse and Utica, there is a pronounced snow belt, brought on by air masses that, moving in from the west, pick up moisture when passing over the Great Lakes.

In northern Maine, the average growing season (that is, the number of days between the last killing frost in the spring and the first in the fall) is approximately 110 days. The number of days increases to over 180 in southern New England and along the southern shores of the Great Lakes, and to 200 days in eastern Maryland. Elevations, of course, are important. At the top of Mount Washington, average temperatures are 20°F. colder than they are at sea level. The tempering influence of the ocean is particularly strong in southern New England, where rain rather than snow is encountered most of the winter. Block Island, a good example of this tempering influence, has a longer average growing season than Washington, D.C.

The Northeast has in recent decades been subject to a number of tropical hurricanes. The 1938 hurricane, the first in the northeastern United States in over a century, caused nearly 500 deaths. It was followed by such others as "Carol" in 1954, "Diane" in 1955, "Donna" in 1960, and "Agnes" in 1972. On several occasions the Northeast has suffered from tornadoes, but they occur in this region less frequently than in the Middle West. In late summer, the coastal areas may be pounded by northeasters—storms with rain and high winds that may continue for several days. But these storms occur rarely, and the Northeast's climate has been favorable to settlement and economic progress. Summers are relatively cool, particularly along the coasts and in the uplands. Winters, although cold in the northern areas, are not extreme. Harbors usually remain open throughout the winter or are blocked by ice for only short periods. Abundant snowfall in New England and New York State facilitates winter sports, while the pronounced spring and fall seasons in the Northeast bring particularly pleasing weather. There are adequate precipitation and growing seasons for both agriculture and the growth of forests throughout practically the entire Northeast, although climatic conditions in other parts of the nation are more suited to the growth of such crops as corn, wheat, and tobacco. There is also considerable underground and surface water, resulting from the precipitation, to supply the water needs of the cities and towns. The frequent changes of weather in the Northeast may, as some writers have claimed, have a stimulating effect on the people who live there. Certainly these changes provide both opportunity for enjoyment and a challenge to day-to-day living, without the extremes of heat, cold, and aridity that are encountered in some other sectors of the United States. The decrease in dependence on agriculture in the Northeast, combined with the increase in urban living and in recreation, means that the climate is, in a sense, more conducive to the inhabitants' way of life today than it was to the colonists' 200 years ago.

VEGETATION AND SOILS

Practically all the Northeast was originally covered by forest. The early settlers began clearing the land for agriculture, and because of requirements for wood, this process continued until very few virgin stands remained in the area. The colonies became important exporters of timber and wood products such as masts, staves, and lumber. The process of deforestation has been augmented by forest fires, hurricanes, floods, and other disasters. Beginning in the latter part of the nineteenth century, agricultural land began to be abandoned, and many areas of the Northeast subsequently returned first to brush and then eventually to forest again. Today the major forest sites of the Northeast are the northern and central parts of Maine, the Adirondacks, the Allegheny Plateau, the coastal plain of southern New Jersey, and smaller upland areas such as the White and Green mountains, the Catskills, and the elongated ridges of the Folded Appalachians.

Needleleaf evergreens, particularly spruce and fir, dominate northern and central Maine, the White Mountains, and the Adirondacks. Throughout central New England, New York State, and north-central Pennsylvania the forests are mixed deciduous and coniferous, with birch, beech, maple, and hemlock predominating. On the sandy soils of Cape Cod, southern Long Island, southern New Jersey, and the Delmarva Peninsula,[2] scrub oak and pitch pine are the leading species. The evergreens are largely absent in the areas of warmer climate in southern New England, most of New Jersey, Pennsylvania, and Maryland, as well as the southern approaches to the Great Lakes. In these areas, oak, hickory, and chestnut are found.

2. The peninsula east of Chesapeake Bay, which contains Delaware, eastern Maryland, and—in its southern end—a portion of Virginia. Its name is derived from the first few letters of each of the three states.

It should be noted, however, that once the virgin forests were removed, the woodland, if given a chance to recover, frequently did not return in the same form. Repeated cuttings have virtually eliminated the stands of hemlock, sugar maple, and yellow birch; in their place such species as oak and white pine have sprouted.

The soils are generally gray-brown podzolic, which means that they are slightly acid, with a low organic content. They are, however, responsive to improvement methods and are capable of good yields if properly fertilized. In northern New England and parts of the Appalachian Highlands, one encounters the true podzols, with their high acidity and very thin humus layer. In the Adirondacks and other mountain areas, soils are extremely shallow; in parts of the coastal plain, they are inclined to be very sandy.

North of the general latitude of New York City the land was once subjected to glaciation, resulting in a surface cover of glacial *till*—that is, a mixture of boulders, small stones, and soil brought down from more northerly areas and deposited by the glaciers. Within the till, many rocks were found that now form the rustic stone walls of this part of the nation. Deposits of sand and gravel are frequently found along with the till, as are poorly drained bog soils associated with the many swamps of the region. Glacial till can be farmed, but generally not as economically as the competing soils of the American Southeast, Midwest, and Far West. Grains, in particular, do better in other environments. By the time of the Civil War, most of America's grain production had moved south and west. Vegetables, cranberries, tree crops, and grass are the principal agricultural uses made today of the glacial soils.

In the nonglaciated parts of the Northeast, soils reflect the underlying rock structure on which they are formed, and they are free of boulders. But here again, the extent of the good soils is limited—by steep slopes, crystalline rocks, or sandy plains. The best soils of the Northeast are those formed on limestone, as in the Great Valley and around Lancaster and York. The red soils of southern Maryland and the alluvial soils of the Connecticut River Valley are also highly productive, particularly for specialty crops such as tobacco and mushrooms.

MINERALS AND POWER FUELS

The minerals and power fuels of the Northeast are not abundant compared to those of some other sectors of the United States. Pennsylvania leads the nation in production of anthracite coal and stands third in that of bituminous coal; from the Niagara Falls–St. Lawrence Seaway area bordering New York State comes about one-twelfth of the developed hydroelectric power of the United States. Other than these resources, however, there is little in the way of commercial value today, except salt, limestone, marble, and granite.

In the days of early industrialization, coal and local iron-ore deposits led to the establishment of an iron and steel industry in eastern Pennsylvania. At Titusville, Pennsylvania, the first commercial oil well was brought in, and a small amount of petroleum is still produced in Pennsylvania and New York State. But most of the minerals and power fuels that the Northeast requires can be imported by sea, pipeline, or rail. Iron ore comes by ship from the Lake Superior region or from South America; copper comes by water from Chile; and petroleum and natural gas are brought in from the Gulf states by ship and pipeline. Bauxite comes by ship and then rail to the aluminum plants of northern New York State. These imports more than make up for the Northeast's shortages in minerals and power fuels.

POPULATION

In colonial times, the Northeast was the population center of the colonies. For over half a century following the Revolution, it continued to have a majority of the new nation's population. Its relative position declined with the gradual opening of the Middle West, and later the West. Millions of immigrants arrived at New York, Boston, and other northeastern ports during the nineteenth and early twentieth centuries. The majority of these immediately moved on to other areas. Since the beginning of the twentieth century, the Northeast's population has fluctuated between 25 and 30 percent of the national total.

In 1970, the area had a total population of 54 million, an increase of 5 million over the 1960 figure. This increase amounted to 10.8 percent during the 1960 to 1970 decade compared with a national average increase of 13.3 percent; it followed a 14.1 percent increase during the 1950s, a time when the national average increase was 18.5 percent. Thus, for over two decades the Northeast has lagged behind the national growth rate. Population statistics for the individual states are given in Table 1.

Three factors particularly stand out in these statistics. The first is the concentration of population in the four states of New York, Pennsylvania, New Jersey, and Massachusetts. The second is the significant growth of population in the 1960 to

TABLE 1. Population in the Northeast

State or District	1970 Population (thousands)	Percent Change 1960–1970	Population per square mile
Maine	987	2.5	32.1
New Hampshire	742	21.5	81.7
Vermont	447	14.1	47.9
Massachusetts	5,704	10.5	727.0
Rhode Island	951	10.5	902.5
Connecticut	3,039	19.6	623.6
New York	18,260	8.4	368.3
New Jersey	7,197	18.2	953.1
Pennsylvania	11,816	4.2	262.3
Delaware	550	22.8	276.5
Maryland	3,939	26.5	396.6
District of Columbia	755	−1.0	12,402.0

1970 decade in Delaware, Maryland, New Jersey, and Connecticut. Practically all of this has resulted from the movement of people into the suburbs of large cities—especially New York, Philadelphia, Baltimore, and Washington. Finally, one should note the population densities in Massachusetts, Rhode Island, Connecticut, and New Jersey, particularly in contrast to northern New England.

The Northeast's share of the total national population has declined in recent years—from 30 percent in 1920 to 26.7 percent in 1970. The biggest differential came in the 1940 to 1950 decade when the Northeast's population grew by less than 11 percent, while the national total increased nearly 14.5 percent. This was the decade of phenomenal growth in the Far West. The statistics for net migration between 1960 and 1970 indicate that over 1 million white persons left the states of Pennsylvania and New York for other areas; 70,000 emigrated from Maine; and 135,000 from the District of Columbia. During the same decade, the Northeast had an in-migration of over 700,000 nonwhites, over half of them going to New York State, with New Jersey and Pennsylvania getting most of the remainder. The minority problem resulting from the influx of these groups into the urban areas represents one of the greatest challenges now facing political and social leaders in this part of the United States.

POPULATION DISTRIBUTION

The history of settlement in the Northeast can be divided into five periods. The first lasted until about 1720. During this time settlement was limited, for the most part, to the seaboard. Orientation was predominantly toward the sea, and many ports were developed; among them, Boston, New Amsterdam (later named New York), Philadelphia, Salem, Nantucket, Newport, New London, and New Haven. Boston at that time was the leading port of the colonies.

During the second period, between 1720 and 1783, movement inland began. Immigrants, such as the Pennsylvania

Dutch, began arriving in large numbers and pushing westward into the Great Valley and along the Mohawk Corridor. Contact with the French outposts was followed by the French and Indian War (1756–1763). After the elimination of the French from the area east of the Mississippi, the westward movement grew in scope. Boston gave way to Philadelphia as the colonies' leading city and port.

During the 1783 to 1815 period, the Northeast continued its expansion both of maritime commerce and inland settlement. Central and western Pennsylvania were settled, along with central New York State and western Maryland. Baltimore grew as a port city; Washington, D.C. was founded; and Philadelphia was surpassed by New York as the country's major city. Many smaller cities began to grow, serving such functions as fishing or whaling towns, trade centers, or foci of new transportation routes. Portsmouth, New Bedford, New London, Newark, Trenton, and Wilmington, along with Harrisburg and the cities along the Mohawk, were among those that began to grow.

The fourth period, from 1815 to 1860, saw a continued growth of secondary centers. This was the era of canal building (Syracuse, Binghamton) and rail construction (Harrisburg, Altoona); but most of the cities that developed in this period did so because of manufacturing—witness the centers along the Merrimack, the Lehigh, and the Delaware rivers. By the time of the Civil War, the predominant settlement pattern of the Northeast had been largely determined.

The fifth period, following eight decades of little growth, is the present one, which dates back to about 1940. This is the era of urbanization—of the movement of people into the larger metropolitan regions but not necessarily to the central cities. Rather, in the past decade, it has been the suburbs and satellite towns about the major cities that have grown rapidly. To illustrate, let us consider the population distribution as it exists in the 1970s.

Over 60 percent of the people in the Northeast live in the belt of urbanized areas stretching from Boston to Washington.

This belt, often referred to as Megalopolis,[3] connects Boston and New York with Philadelphia, Baltimore, and Washington and is followed by a main line of the Penn-Central Railroad and by U.S. Route 1 and parallel highways. In this region are located 21 of the 30 cities in the Northeast having populations exceeding 100,000.

The existence of a Boston-Washington urban axis shows the extremely urbanized nature of much of the population of the Northeast. About 80 percent of the total population of the area resides in urban areas (that is, cities and towns having populations of 2,500 or over). In New Jersey, the percentage of the state's total population that is classed as urban is 88.9, and in Rhode Island it is 87.1. Yet statistics such as these reveal only part of the situation.

The Boston-Washington axis might be thought of as divided into four subregions: southern New England, Metropolitan New York, the Delaware Valley, and the Baltimore-Washington conurbation. In many of the larger metropolises of these subregions, the population of the cities actually declined in the 1960 to 1970 decade, while there was considerable growth in the outlying districts.

In southeastern New England, the urbanized areas focus on Boston. It is the sixteenth largest city in the nation, with a population of 640,000. The Boston metropolitan district—which includes such nearby cities as Brookline, Cambridge, and Somerville—has a population of 2.9 million. This places it eighth in population in the United States' metropolitan areas. There has been a pronounced population movement in the past two decades away from Boston itself, a pattern that is also repeated in other metropolitan districts of southeastern

3. See Jean Gottmann's *Megalopolis* (New York: The Twentieth Century Fund, 1961). In Gottmann's pioneering work, the limits of Megalopolis included western Massachusetts, Ulster and Sullivan counties in New York State, Pennsylvania as far west as Scranton and Harrisburg, all of Delaware and Maryland, and northern Virginia. The book should be read by all persons interested in the northeastern seaboard.

New England, such as Worcester, Providence-Pawtucket, Fall River, and Lawrence-Haverhill. In southwestern New England there is no one large urban center but rather a series of cities in the Connecticut River Valley and along the shore of Long Island Sound. Beginning with Springfield, Massachusetts, this area includes Hartford, New Haven, Bridgeport, and Stamford. In southwestern Connecticut, within a commuting radius of New York City, some townships more than doubled in population between 1940 and 1970.

The Metropolitan New York subregion contains over 15 million people, or nearly one-third the total population of the Northeast. The New York City area alone has 10 million people, while in northeastern New Jersey the major population centers are Newark, Jersey City, Paterson-Passaic, and Trenton. Here, as in southwestern Connecticut, the growth rate of suburban areas since the late 1930s has been extremely high.

Philadelphia, with a population of 2 million, is the nation's fourth largest city. Its metropolitan district includes Camden, Chester, and a number of smaller towns. To the southwest, on the Delaware River, is Wilmington. Within the combined Philadelphia-Wilmington region are close to 5 million people.

The Baltimore-Washington conurbation has considerably fewer people than the Philadelphia-New York area. Baltimore, with a population of 900,000, ranks seventh among the cities of the United States, while Washington, with 760,000 people, ranks ninth. Neither city, however, has yet built up a surrounding belt of satellite cities. Baltimore's metropolitan district has only half the population of the Boston metropolitan area and is even smaller than the metropolitan area of Washington.

Outside the Boston-Washington corridor, there are some 10 million other persons in the Northeast living in metropolitan districts. The majority of these districts are located in one of three general areas. The first area is the Mohawk-Ontario Plain lowlands. This district contains a string of urban areas including Albany, Utica, Syracuse, Rochester, Buffalo, and Erie, together with many smaller cities. Over 3.5 million people live in these metropolitan regions. Another 2.5 million live in the metropolitan district of Pittsburgh. Nearly 2 million more live in the various metropolitan areas of east-central Pennsylvania including Scranton, Wilkes-Barre, Allentown, Reading, Harrisburg, Lancaster, and York. Beyond these three urban agglomerations are a number of scattered metropolitan areas in the Northeast, none of them of major size. These include Johnstown and Altoona in west-central Pennsylvania; Binghamton in southern New York; Atlantic City; New London, Connecticut; and Portland, Maine.

During the 1960 to 1970 decade there was a pronounced movement of people away from many of the rural areas. Of the 245 counties in the Northeast, 45 actually lost population during the ten-year period. Nine counties in northern New England declined in population, as did seven counties in the hard-coal district of eastern Pennsylvania and in east-central New York State. In western Pennsylvania and westernmost Maryland, 19 counties lost population due to the deteriorating conditions of the coal industry. The remaining 10 counties with population decreases during the decade consisted largely of central cities, such as Boston, New York, Philadelphia, Baltimore, and Washington. It should be noted that of the 45 Northeastern counties that lost population during the 1960 to 1970 decade, 30 of them also lost population in the 1950 to 1960 decade.

Seventy Northeastern counties, on the other hand, gained more rapidly in population than the national average between 1960 and 1970. Most of these are located along the Boston-Washington corridor. This area of rapid increase includes a majority of the Rhode Island counties and nearly all of Connecticut, southeastern New York State, New Jersey, southeastern Pennsylvania, Delaware, and eastern Maryland. In suburbia, or perhaps suburbia and exurbia, population increases have been high. Ocean County, New Jersey, north of Atlantic City, had an increase of 93 percent during the decade; Prince George's County, Maryland, (adjoining Washington) increased 85 percent; and Putnam County, New York (about 50 miles north of New York City) grew by 79 percent. Rockland County, New York, which is situated across the Hudson from Westchester, increased by 68 percent. The increase was the same in Suffolk County, which is the easternmost county of Long Island. It is interesting to note that Westchester and Nassau counties, which are adjacent to New York City, did not even keep pace with the national average for the decade's growth.

There were high increases for other Maryland counties peripheral to Washington and Baltimore, particularly Montgomery, Howard, Ann Arundel, and Harford. Sussex and Morris counties, west and northwest of New York City; Washington County in southern Rhode Island; Barnstable County (Cape Cod) and Plymouth County, Massachusetts, also increased considerably in population above the national average during the decade, as did Rockingham, New Hampshire's coastal county, and Burlington County, New Jersey, which lies northeast of Philadelphia.

The general shift in the population of the Northeast is not just a phenomenon of the past few years, but part of a trend that has been going on for considerable time. Some of the rural counties have been losing population for three or four decades. The political impact of these population changes will be covered in Chapter 2. It is noted there that the Northeast has declined in political strength relative to other parts of the nation through the recent net loss of four representatives in Congress.

The immigration into the cities of low-income groups has had both political and social implications. New York City, for example, in 1970 had 846,000 Puerto Ricans, or over 80 percent of the total Puerto Rican population in the United States. These people tend to be segregated in ghettos and to be offered only the poorest paying jobs in the city. There were 105,000 Puerto Ricans in the New Jersey area west of New York City, and 45,000 more in the greater Philadelphia area. Over 70 percent of Washington is nonwhite; over half the people of Newark are nonwhite; and more than one-third of those in Baltimore and Philadelphia are nonwhite. The influx of nonwhites is largely a phenomenon of the past three decades, another element of change in this area. And the problem of segregation is by no means limited to the southeastern

United States. Although many of the nonwhites of the Northeastern cities are entitled to vote (and usually vote Democratic), they have been generally unsuccessful in breaking residential restrictions and those in the field of employment.

Despite the influx of low-income groups to the cities, the people of the Northeast are, on the average, among the wealthiest in the nation. The District of Columbia leads the country in per capita personal income, followed by Connecticut and New York. New Jersey is in fifth place behind Nevada; and Delaware, Maryland, and Massachusetts are in ninth, tenth, and eleventh places, respectively. Only Maine, New Hampshire, Vermont, and Rhode Island are below the national per capita average. These income levels reflect, in part, the occupational pattern of the Northeast. In a total labor force of over 21 million, the majority are employed in manufacturing, in services, and in the professions, where annual salaries tend to be high.

2 The Impact of Urbanization and Technology

Within the Northeast, the twin forces of urbanization and technology have combined to produce radical changes in the landscape and in the ways of life of a great number of the inhabitants. Technology has made possible the redesigning of important parts of the central cities and the suburban sprawl out into the surrounding countryside, as well as the relocation of industries away from the urban core. It is continuing to revolutionize agriculture and coal mining in the Northeast, to reroute major transportation links, and to provide new forms of resource use for the rising demands of the Northeast's population. As one of the technological centers of the world, this region has reacted strongly to innovations. In this chapter some of the direct and indirect implications of changing technology and settlement patterns will be considered.

There are various ways of measuring the degree of urbanization in the Northeast. The 1970 census lists over 43 million people, or 80 percent of the population, as urban—a percentage figure that is 6 percent above the national average. Some of the cities and towns, however, are far from the major metropolitan centers; thus, in a sense, they do not share in many of the characteristic problems and trends of the larger urban centers. A more meaningful figure would be the total of the population living in the Northeast's Standard Metropolitan

Statistical Areas. These areas contain at least one central city with 50,000 inhabitants or more or a city having at least 25,000 people that, together with the population of contiguous places having a population density of at least 1,000 persons per square mile, constitutes for general economic and social purposes a single community with a combined population of at least 50,000. The county or counties within which the city and contiguous places are located must have a total population of at least 75,000. Based on these criteria, less than 20 percent of the total population of the Northeast lives outside the large urban centers.

The larger cities of the Northeast are, for the most part, old established areas with changing economic bases and population structures. The central districts of Boston, Philadelphia, Baltimore, Pittsburgh, and others have become ill-suited to modern transport needs. Industries have moved away—sometimes to outlying districts, but often away from the area completely. Population patterns have changed. First, many of the well-to-do moved to the suburbs. Then came the exodus of the middle class, along with the gradual return of some of the wealthier to new high-rise apartments and an influx of the poor into the central cities. If one were to generalize about the major problems faced by these larger urban areas, they might be classified under the following headings:

1) The competition for space.
2) Obsolescence and the need for renewal and rehabilitation.
3) New transportation requirements.
4) The search for water supplies and recreation areas.
5) The need for electric power.
6) The political impact of population shifts.
7) The rise of technological unemployment.
8) Increased pressures on the coastal zone.

THE COMPETITION FOR SPACE

The first point to note about most of the metropolitan areas of the Northeast is the restricted size of the major cities themselves, a holdover from the past when municipal boundaries were delimited. Philadelphia's nearly 2 million people are crowded into 127 square miles. Boston's 640,000 live in 48 square miles, and in New York, 7.9 million people reside in 315 square miles. The average density on Manhattan Island is 68,000 persons per square mile; but on Staten Island, which is another borough, it is less than 7 percent of this figure. This indicates a potential settlement frontier for New Yorkers, now that the Verrazano-Narrows Bridge to Brooklyn has been opened. To illustrate contrasting metropolitan planning, the land areas of these cities might be compared with the 455 square miles of the city of Los Angeles or Houston's 328 square miles.

Within the central cities, competition for space is an obvious fact. Space must be found for the great number of inhabitants to live and work. This means space for dwellings, places of employment, public and private services (including recreation), and transportation facilities. While relatively few persons living in the central cities travel daily to the suburbs for work, there is always a substantial influx of workers each day into the downtown areas from outlying districts. Since the total acreage of the central cities is limited, competition for space may become exceedingly keen and land values rise accordingly.

One answer to the space problem, of course, may be vertical construction, as in the new World Trade Center. The Wall Street district of New York and, more recently, the city's midtown area have succeeded in packing enormous daily working populations into a small amount of horizontal space. The business districts of Philadelphia, Pittsburgh, Boston, Baltimore, and Newark have also been extended skyward. New York has led in the construction of high-rise apartments for its central city inhabitants and, again, Philadelphia and other cities have followed suit, although on a far more restricted scale. The city of the future might well be studded with business or residential skyscrapers, but only a part of the space competition problem would then be solved.

Most of the inhabitants of the central cities are unaffected by the high-rise apartments. They live in two- to eight-story apartments or in row houses. If their homes are razed because of urban renewal or some other project, they seldom leave the city, and only a few of the displaced move into the new quarters erected on the site. The rest must find homes in other older apartments. It has already been noted that in most of the cities there has been an influx of low-income families who tend to settle in the central districts. What of the needs of these people for services and for transportation? Their recreation requirements, for example, may be greater than those of the inhabitants of a decade or more ago, so that demands for public parks and playgrounds will increase rather than diminish.

Consider the case of transportation. The exodus of much of the middle class to the suburbs has meant greater demands for highways going into the cities, for parking facilities, and for more realistic traffic patterns in downtown areas. But express highways are enormous consumers of space, even if they are elevated, and parking garages more than a few floors in height are very expensive to operate.

The competition for space in downtown areas has also affected institutions such as universities and hospitals. Urban universities face constant needs for expansion. The University of Pennsylvania and Temple University in Philadelphia; George Washington University in Washington; Boston University; Columbia, New York University, and the City University of New York; Brown in Providence; Johns Hopkins in Baltimore; and the Universities of Pittsburgh and Rochester— these and many others face a never-ending search for urban space in which to grow and develop. Some of these institutions have medical schools and hospitals attached to them. In addition, each of the urban areas of the Northeast has one or more city hospitals with space problems.

Competition for space is, of course, a relative quantity. Every city has within its limits vacant or unused space, but this is generally in undesirable locations. One goal of urban planners is to formulate programs for maximum utilization of such space by relocating or improving various urban functions. But such programs may involve large expenditures of public or private funds and can only be carried out within the framework of a major urban-renewal program.

Out in the suburbs the competition for space is also intense. Although much of the land must go for house lots, there are also demands for stores, schools, parks and playgrounds, municipal dumps, sewage disposal units, and so on. Industries moving to the suburbs may desire large areas for construction. Farms may still exist beyond the city limits, along with estates, religious institutions, and private schools and colleges. Through the suburbs, arterial highways may be built to connect with the downtown areas. And in the suburbs and beyond, there is the constant need for obtaining and conserving fresh water supplies, both for the suburban users and for the city itself.

It must be remembered that settlement and the use of land in the Northeast has had a long history of development and that as urban areas expand outward, they frequently do so at the expense of land already undergoing intensive utilization. That is, the urban fringe may come to incorporate smaller cities and towns that have existed as independent units for a long time. It may also encompass productive farmland or recreational areas. As the urban fringes of adjacent metropolises crawl closer toward one another, there is a growing need for setting aside some fairly extensive stretches of undeveloped land between them for future recreational use. Such a need is behind the Green Acres program, in which federal funds are used along with those of state and local areas to set aside land for the future. Certainly along the Boston-Washington and Hudson-Mohawk corridors there are relatively few extensive empty areas left in which land is inexpensive and in little demand.

OBSOLESCENCE AND THE NEED FOR URBAN RENEWAL

Since the cities of the Northeast are among the oldest in the nation, the problem of obsolescence is a very real one. One might think, for example, of the street pattern of downtown Boston, where the arrangement of colonial paths has been preserved to plague today's motorists; of the dilapidated row houses of Baltimore; or of the abandoned mills in Fall River and New Bedford. One might consider the worn-out tenements in Harlem or Brooklyn's Bedford-Stuyvesant area, in south Boston, in south Philadelphia, or in southeast Washington; or visit smaller, once-prosperous cities like Wilkes-Barre, Utica, or Woonsocket for signs of obsolescence. What has characterized so many of the cities of the Northeast during the past decades has been not only dilapidated buildings, empty factories, and absurd traffic patterns but also an overwhelming aura of decay—the exodus of the upper- and middle-income groups to suburbia, the decline in commerce and industry, and the steady deterioration of the tax base and hence of the cities' financial positions.

This decay shows itself in many forms, including the lack of quality metropolitan newspapers; the corrupt character of municipal governments; and the lack of service facilities, such as first-class hotels and restaurants, legitimate theaters, or symphony orchestras. The struggle to maintain the central city as the focus of the economic, social, and cultural forces of the surrounding areas has too often been an unsuccessful one in the Northeast. Former centers such as Trenton, New Haven, Hartford, and even Boston and Philadelphia are frequently bypassed in favor of New York as a place for shopping, for cultural activities, and in which to live and work.

Faced with this specter of decay, the cities of the Northeast have been forced to take stock of themselves and to inaugurate long-range programs for urban renewal. These programs involve the expenditure of funds from both the public and private sectors. They may center on slum clearance and redevelopment, or on rehabilitation in which improvements are made to already existing structures. The rate at which renewal programs have been carried out varies widely from city to city. Some areas such as Pittsburgh, Philadelphia, New Haven, New York, Albany, and Boston have made great strides in the past twenty-five years; others have been considerably slower. What is important is that these various programs have had a significant impact on urban development in the Northeast and will have even greater effects in the years to come.

The key to the whole urban-renewal movement is the Housing Act of 1949. This act authorized the federal government to pay to cities at least two-thirds of the difference between the cost of acquiring and clearing a particular area of the city and the price the land would bring if sold to a private developer. Originally designed as a slum-clearance project, this act has been considerably expanded and modified, so as to apply to the redevelopment of downtown, nonresidential sectors of cities as well as to the rehabilitation of old houses and points of interest. Equally important has been the stimulus provided by federal urban-renewal action to the outlay of private funds for redevelopment in the cities of the Northeast. Insurance companies, banks, industrial corporations, and individual investors have more than matched federal, state, and municipal funds in the renewal of these urban areas.

Pittsburgh was one of the first cities of the Northeast to draw up and execute a major renewal program. In 1944, city officials proposed a plan whereby state and municipal funds would be joined with those of private investors to clear up the Golden Triangle at the junction of the Allegheny and Monongahela rivers in downtown Pittsburgh. Six years later, the Gateway Center project was begun in this area by the Equitable Life Insurance Company on land adjoining the new 36-acre Point State Park, which was being developed by the state of Pennsylvania. Pittsburgh itself was already instituting measures to cut down the smoke and soot, which for so long had engulfed the city, and was beginning the construction of a new civic center. Eventually other private corporations—such as Alcoa, U.S. Steel, IBM, and the Mellon Bank—began investing in the city's expanding renewal program.

Another early leader in renewal was Philadelphia, where since 1952 government and private funds have been spent on one of the most comprehensive urban programs in the United States. Among other things, Philadelphia has constructed a $120 million Penn Center in the central city, with office buildings, a hotel, and sunken gardens and pedestrian malls. The city has also built a series of high-rise apartments in a former slum area overlooking the Delaware River, a half-billion-dollar Market Street East project involving reconstruction of major retailing areas, and a 2,500-acre shopping center in southwest Philadelphia in an area formerly consisting of marshes and junkyards. Somewhat later, Boston began development of a $180 million Government Center in the old Scollay Square area along with the privately financed $200 million Prudential Center complete with a 52-story building and the first new hotel to be built in the city in over 25 years. The Prudential Building was subsequently joined by an even taller John Hancock Tower.

Albany has a one-billion-dollar South Mall project; Stamford, a $200 million downtown urban-renewal project; and New Haven, a program of similar magnitude. Hartford has a Civic Center Plaza, which includes a hotel, coliseum, and exhibition hall; Syracuse has a federal office building and combined office-cultural center; and Washington has the new L'Enfant Plaza. Baltimore's Charles Center and its $450 million redevelopment of 240 acres surrounding the inner harbor are indicative of the city's renewal activities. Newark, Providence, and Buffalo also have important urban-renewal projects, as do Rochester, Paterson, Wilmington, Scranton, and Jersey City.

New York City is in a constant state of urban renewal. Recently, the city completed its $700 million, 1,350-foot, twin-towered World Trade Center in lower Manhattan, the world's tallest building for a short time, until it was eclipsed by Chicago's Sears Tower. It will soon start construction on a $100 million Convention Center, and other projects are already underway, such as the 100-acre Battery Park City, with 16,000 apartments and 6 million square feet of office space, the Manhattan Landing project on the lower East River, with 7,000 apartments and 8 million square feet of office space, and the Waterside Housing complex, also on the East River, with a two-acre public plaza and 1,500 apartments.

But impressive as these great downtown projects may be,

there is an even greater need for slum clearance and rehabilitation projects in the Northeastern cities. Baltimore, having rehabilitated a nonwhite district containing 2,000 dilapidated homes, has now begun a $200 million Coldspring project, which will provide 3,800 middle- and upper-income housing units. Philadelphia's Franklin Town is a privately financed, $200 million redevelopment of a mid-city site to provide 4,000 residential units. Washington has spent more than $500 million on its 560-acre Southwest Development Area project, while New York's Westside Urban-Renewal Project involves 20 blocks and some 34,000 people. A race is on between decay and renewal, both in the low-income residential areas and in the business districts of the cities of the Northeast.

Since 1965, residential housing in New York City has been in a state of growing disaster. An estimated 500,000 families are living in substandard or seriously deteriorating housing, and 30,000 units a year are said to be lost through abandonment, fires, and demolition. In Harlem alone one-quarter of the housing units are badly deteriorated and in need of replacement. Yet in contrast to the estimated 66,000 new housing units a year that are needed, less than 20,000 are being built. The city recently dedicated the 5,900-unit Starrett City in Brooklyn—a project that was in the planning stage for ten years. At about the same time, Mayor Beame announced that he was hopeful of receiving federal assistance for the construction of 24,000 new and rehabilitated apartments per year over a three-year period for low-income families, under the Federal Housing and Community Development Act of 1974. A combination of scarce mortgage money and high-interest rates have contributed to a sharp decline in housing construction both in New York and in other cities of the Northeast.

It is still too early to assess the impact of urban-renewal programs on the cities of the Northeast. Certainly Pittsburgh, Philadelphia, New York, Boston, Hartford, and other centers have benefitted from their new business and civic centers, which were designed to bring white-collar jobs back into the downtown areas. New high-income apartments will accelerate the move of the well-to-do back into the central cities, while slum clearance and rehabilitation projects will benefit great numbers of low-income families. There will be new parks, new highways, new hotels, shopping centers, parking areas, and other service facilities for the commuter and the out-of-town visitor. But the basic question is still to be answered: Will these new developments lead to economic and social revitalization of the cities and to a growth of confidence on the part of investors so far as the cities' productive functions are concerned?

NEW TRANSPORTATION REQUIREMENTS

The urbanized areas of the Northeast face staggering problems of public and private transportation both within and between urban centers. For the sake of this discussion, transportation requirements will be considered under the following four headings: highway traffic, rail transportation, air transportation, and water traffic.

Mention has already been made of the archaic street patterns in the downtown sections of such cities as Boston, Philadelphia, and Baltimore. Officials here and in other centers have resorted to such devices as one-way traffic, off-street parking, and bans on left turns during certain hours to cope with congestion problems. The fact is, however, that as more workers in the city move out to the suburbs, traffic problems become worse rather than better.

Washington furnishes a good example. Although much of the downtown section was planned in advance, it was not planned for the automobile era, and the complicated system of circles and diagonal streets results in considerable congestion during rush hours. Washington's suburbs have spread out in all directions, yet connections with the downtown areas are poor. Only four bridges span the Potomac between the District and Virginia; one of these, the Chain Bridge, is too far north and too small to be of great value. Motorists approaching Washington from the northeast have miles of congested city streets on which to travel before reaching the center city.

Baltimore has an expressway crossing its southeastern corner, but the highway does not serve its major suburban areas, rather, it carries through-traffic between Washington and Philadelphia. Another expressway, running north from Baltimore, handles traffic from that direction, but from west and southeast of Baltimore there are poor connections with the downtown area. Philadelphia's Schuylkill Expressway, Pittsburgh's Penn Lincoln Parkway, and Boston's John F. Fitzgerald Expressway are other examples of high-speed arteries giving access to central areas. Although these provide the motorist with ingress and egress to the cities, they have two drawbacks: 1) they make possible even greater amounts of traffic in the downtown areas, and 2) they soon become inadequate, as evidenced by Boston's Fitzgerald Expressway—even before its completion date plans were being made for additional lanes.

Nearly 750,000 automobiles enter Manhattan's business district each working day. The island is connected to the east with Brooklyn and Queens by five bridges and two tunnels and to the north with the Bronx by nine bridges. But most traffic moving to and from Manhattan is handicapped by the fact that only two tunnels and one bridge connect to the west with New Jersey and by the shortage of expressways leading to the approaches to the island.

The problem of expressways involves not only New York City itself but also Connecticut and New Jersey, as well as Nassau and Suffolk counties on Long Island and the New York State counties north of the city. Routes such as the New York State and New England thruways, the Northern and Southern State parkways, the Long Island Expressway and the Sunrise Highway, and the Pulaski Skyway funnel traffic into the city. The coordination of these highways and the planning for their enlargement or for supplementing them by other routes, however, involves a considerable number of governmental agencies in the Greater New York area. Then, too, there is the problem of traffic to and from New England or eastern Long Island that seeks to bypass Manhattan or to cross it with a minimum of interruptions. One outer-highway net connects the New England Thruway with the New Jersey Turnpike over the Hudson, about fifteen miles north of Manhattan Island. From the western end of the bridge, motorists may proceed by the New York State Thruway and the Garden State Parkway to connect with the southbound New Jersey Turnpike.

Two other routes follow the New England Thruway to the northeastern boundary of New York City. From here, one system passes west via the Cross Bronx Expressway and northernmost Manhattan Island to connect with the George Washington Bridge over the Hudson and the New Jersey Turnpike, while the other passes southeast via the Throgs Neck Bridge over the East River to eastern Queens and the Long Island belt system. The completion of the Verrazano-Narrows Bridge between Staten Island and Brooklyn provided an express route between the New Jersey Turnpike and the Long Island belt system that bypasses Manhattan; at the same time, it provided convenient connections through Brooklyn between Staten Island and Manhattan.

In New York City, as in the other metropolitan areas, city officials are continually planning for new transportation facilities, even though the completion date may be 15 to 20 years away. Arterial highways, bridges, and tunnels, for example, must be planned for and specifications prepared. Approval must be obtained from the necessary legislative and executive bodies (often involving more than one level of government), funding must be secured, and the necessary land appropriated before any construction can begin. The original planning must be based on assessments of transportation needs many years hence. In the case of New York City, highway facilities have not kept up with demands, nor are there indications that within the next few years the gap between supply and demand will close.

The metropolitan areas of the Northeast are interconnected by an ever-increasing system of expressways. Boston to Washington, Boston to Buffalo, Pittsburgh to New York—these and other distances are now covered by high-speed routes such as the Massachusetts, Connecticut, New Jersey, and Pennsylvania turnpikes, the New York State Thruway, and the John F. Kennedy Expressway in northeastern Maryland. Older routes such as Connecticut's Merritt and Wilbur Cross parkways or Boston's Route 128 are now considered out-of-date, and already programs are underway for enlarging some of the newer highways, such as the New Jersey Turnpike (whose enlargement was recently completed), to handle the continually expanding traffic. Along with this has come the construction of second bridges at major crossing points. For example, the Chesapeake Bay Bridge at Annapolis and the Delaware Memorial Bridge below Wilmington now have a parallel span. New bridge construction is also underway for Connecticut Turnpike traffic at New London.

Expressways have been built to link Philadelphia to Watertown, New York (via I-81); Boston with Houlton, Maine (I-95); Albany with the Canadian border (I-87); and New York City with Ohio through central Pennsylvania (I-80). Interstate 93 connects Boston with Concord, New Hampshire, and the Canadian border north of St. Johnsbury, Vermont; I-89 runs from Concord northwest through Burlington; while I-91 extends northward from New Haven through the Connecticut River Valley. Plans are still at least under consideration for a 23-mile island-hopping span across the entrance to the Long Island Sound from Orient Point, Long Island, to Old Saybrook, Connecticut, thereby creating an additional connection between southeastern New England and the areas south of New York City. As these systems become interconnected, they form a magnificent network of high-speed roads—a network that is being linked through Virginia and Ohio with other systems of the nation.

But as more and more traffic is channeled along these limited-access routes, what happens to the areas served by the older highways, such as U.S. 1, 20, and 22? What happens to the tourist facilities that exist there—the cabins and motels and restaurants? What happens to the towns themselves—such as Auburn and Geneva, New York, Lewistown, Pennsylvania, and Willimantic, Connecticut—which once served as overnight stopping points for motorists and truckers? The relocation of highways has seriously affected their transient business. On the other hand, the new expressways are creating new transportation foci, such as Syracuse and Harrisburg, where both trucking and overnight lodging facilities are expanding. Relocation and concentration seem to be major trends resulting from the establishment of the Northeast's system of superhighways.

Urbanization has also brought serious problems in the field of rail transportation. The existence of high-speed turnpikes virtually paralleling the railroad right-of-way has meant ruinous competition for passenger traffic between the trains on one hand and buses and private automobiles on the other. But the railroads are beginning to reduce travel time. Amtrak's minimum scheduled running time between New York and Washington is now 3 hours and 4 minutes, over an hour less than the fastest express bus. A new New York-Albany-Buffalo train now completes the 432-mile trip in eight and a half hours.

The problems of the Northeastern railroads are complex. In 1968, the Pennsylvania and the New York Central railroads combined into the Penn-Central system. Prior to that time the Long Island Railroad, a commuter line owned by the Pennsylvania, was sold to New York State and has since been operated as a publically owned line. In 1969, the bankrupt New Haven Railroad joined the Penn-Central, but a year later the entire system was in bankruptcy, threatening both passenger and freight service along the Northeast corridor.

In May, 1971, the National Railroad Passenger Corporation (Amtrak) began operating nationwide, utilizing the tracks of existing lines. It was designed as an intercity passenger carrier, leaving commuter and freight operations to the individual railroads. Nearly half the costs of Amtrak's services are borne by the taxpayer; in 1974, the annual federal subsidy to Amtrak was close to $200 million.

Although massive federal aid was poured into the ailing Penn-Central system, it failed to respond. Meanwhile, other northeastern railroads, such as the combined Erie-Lackawanna and the Boston and Maine, also went into bankruptcy. Thus it was, in January, 1974, that President Nixon signed into law the Regional Rail Reorganization Act, establishing the

United States Railway Association to plan and finance a streamlined rail network for 17 eastern states. The Association, in November, 1975, created the Consolidated Rail Corporation (Conrail), which acquired the assets of seven bankrupt railroad lines—the Penn-Central, Reading, Lehigh Valley, Central of New Jersey, Lehigh and Hudson River, the tiny Ann Arbor Railroad of Michigan, and parts of the Erie-Lackawanna system. In so doing, Conrail acquired equipment and other assets valued at over $7 billion, but it also acquired a network losing over $1 million per day. Some 21,000 miles of track and about 90,000 workers come under Conrail's jurisdiction, and immediate plans were to drastically reduce the extent of track in operation to about 17,000 miles. Initially, Conrail will own the rights of way used by Amtrak and will operate rail commuter lines in the New York metropolitan area and elsewhere.

In order to avoid the aura of monopoly, the federal government will also assist in developing a private company, built around the Chessie System and including parts of the Erie-Lackawanna Railroad. Conrail will eventually account for about 37 percent of the region's net ton miles annually; the Chessie system for 32 percent; the Norfolk and Western, 21 percent; and smaller solvent lines, about 10 percent. Among the lines in the Northeast not in bankruptcy are the Delaware and Hudson, the Maine Central, the Rutland, the Bangor and Aroostook, the Providence and Worcester, and the Norwich and Worcester. These, for the most part, carry only freight.

There are plans for Amtrak to institute high-speed trains, under a proposed $1 billion grant program, for track construction on 12 corridor routes, as well as for the purchase of new equipment. Over one-quarter of the total funding would be for the Boston-Washington route. Train speeds would average 110 miles per hour, cutting the Boston-New York travel time from its present four-hour minimum to two hours and one-half and cutting the New York-Washington time from three hours to two. It would require considerable improvement of trackage, particularly between New York and Boston. It would also eliminate grade crossings and bypass the crowded freight yards that force through-trains to slow down in the vicinity of cities.

Another type of railroad problem involves the commuter services. With increased costs and high rental fees, railroads have found that commuting systems are consistent money losers. Amtrak, as noted earlier, did not take over the commuting systems of the railroads with which they have been involved. Although many plans have been offered for dealing with the commuter problem, the answer to the funding issue would seem to lie—as has been the case with intercity rail travel—with public agencies. Boston's Massachusetts Bay Transit Authority has been subsidizing commuter service, although largely on an *ad hoc* basis, and waiting for some final resolution to be worked out. New York State has been underwriting the costs of the Long Island Railroad, and both New York and Connecticut contribute to the Penn-Central commuter system from New Haven to New York. In the light of the gasoline crisis, the willingness of the federal government to assist cities in developing rapid transit facilities, and the expressed desire of urban officials in the Northeast to retain white-collar jobs within the cities, there appears to be little reason to abandon public assistance for the rail commuter lines, although the details of a long-term plan for regulating such assistance are still unresolved.

Along with the issue of rail service is that of rapid transit within the metropolitan areas themselves. Boston, which built the nation's first subway, has undertaken a $400 million modernization program. New York has begun the construction of a Second Avenue subway, and Pittsburgh is planning a $230 million rapid transit system linking the central city with the suburbs. Baltimore has begun work on a $1.1 billion bus-rail rapid transit system—Phase 1 of which will provide a subway-aerial service to the south beyond Friendship Airport and to the northeast into Baltimore County. Washington's 98-mile-long Metro, which combines both subway and surface lines, is to cost nearly $4 billion and will provide considerable relief to that traffic-scarred city. As in the case of Baltimore, service will be provided from the principal airport to the center city.

The Urban Mass Transportation Act of 1970 provides for a maximum of $10 billion over a twelve-year period to help U.S. cities revitalize their bus and subway facilities. The federal funds are to pay two-thirds of costs, the other third to come from local sources. Four years after the act came into force, a Federal Mass Transit Bill was enacted, providing $11.8 billion additional funds over a six-year period for the hard-pressed cities. About one-sixth of the annual appropriations for each city would normally go for operating costs—a feature not appearing in the earlier act. But municipal governments would be permitted each year to utilize up to half the funds allocated to capital expenditures for operating subsidies, providing these operating funds are replaced the following year. Such federal action should serve as a catalyst to several of the Northeast's stalled or slow-moving rapid transit programs, including New York's Second Avenue line, the 63rd Street crosstown line to Queens, and the rail link from Kennedy Airport to Pennsylvania Station.

Air transportation is very well developed in this part of the United States. The principal problem involves the location and functioning of airports. Boston's Logan Airport is directly across the harbor from the downtown section, and Washington's National Airport is less than two miles from the central city. In both cases there is easy access to the airport from the city; but pilots must contend with poor visibility and tall buildings close to the field, while city residents often complain of the noise of low-flying planes. To cope with this, Washington has constructed its mammoth Dulles International Airport, located nearly 30 miles west of the city in Virginia, but this field concentrates largely on international flights.

At Philadelphia and Buffalo, the municipal airports are at the outskirts of the city, where visibility is often bad but where potential navigation hazards and nuisance to residents is lessened. Baltimore's Friendship Airport is located in open country about nine miles from the central city and connected to it by excellent highways. In this case, Baltimore has profited from the fact that there has not been pronounced urban expansion southwest of the city.

The Northeast is peppered with commercial airports. Some, such as those at Worcester and Binghamton, are built on the tops of hills to improve visibility. The Greater Pittsburgh Airport is also on high ground, about 17 miles from the downtown area. Between the Northeast's airports fly a number of smaller airlines—Allegheny and Pilgrim to name two—as well as many of the larger systems, such as American, Delta, Eastern, and TWA. On some of the short flights, the airlines must compete with surface transportation with respect to time. A flight from Philadelphia to New York, for example, may take only forty minutes, as compared to one and a half hours by train; but to the flight time must be added that of getting to and from the airports.

There is also the problem of what is sometimes called the "traffic shadow," particularly in cities such as Philadelphia, Baltimore, and Providence. Long-distance flights tend to congregate at particular airports where interconnections and concentrated facilities are possible. Washington, New York, and Boston are more often points of termination and departure, both for overseas and for long domestic flights, than are the intermediate airports. Baltimore's Friendship Airport served for a time as the jet airport for Washington as well. Indeed, it could have continued to do so for a considerable time, but there were pressures in the District of Columbia for the construction of a separate airfield. Although the new Dulles Airport is only slightly closer to downtown Washington than is the Friendship, it tended for a time to draw off much of Friendship's traffic. But Friendship now seems to have recovered most of its former business. Hillsgrove Airport, south of Providence, serves the entire state of Rhode Island, but it is very much within the shadow of Boston, forty-five miles away.

New York City is a nightmare to air-traffic planners. The area is served by three main airports—Newark, LaGuardia, and Kennedy International (formerly Idlewild). Newark Airport, 15 miles southeast of lower Manhattan, is adjacent to the cities of Elizabeth and Newark and suffers almost continuous visibility difficulties because of the industrial developments near it. LaGuardia, which is less than half as far from Manhattan, has been hopelessly overcrowded. Kennedy International is located in southern Queens and handles most of the international traffic for New York City. Here, too, facilities are inadequate for projected traffic within the next decade, and residents in Queens and surrounding areas complain frequently about the noise of the jets.

Some years ago the New York Port Authority, which operates the three airports, began a survey of potential sites farther away from New York for the construction of a new jetport that could divert some of the larger planes away from the immediate areas of the city. One requirement of the site was that it have reasonable accessibility to Manhattan; another was that it be located so that its traffic did not interfere with the existing traffic patterns of other airports. There were also the problems of available space and of suitability of the terrain for airport construction. Officials of the Port Authority considered several locations away from New York: Suffolk County in eastern Long Island; Rockland and Orange counties, 50 to 75 miles northwest of Manhattan; directly west of the city; and south, in New Jersey, toward Philadelphia and Atlantic City. But nearly everywhere they were blocked—by hilly terrain, competing traffic systems, unavailable land, or inadequate accessibility to New York City. Near Morristown, New Jersey, 25 miles west of Manhattan, they found what seemed a desirable site in an undeveloped swampy area—sufficiently removed from Newark Airport traffic yet accessible to New York. But the area was also a site of high-income residences, and sufficient pressure was put on the New Jersey state government to bring about the passage of a bill specifically prohibiting the construction of a jetport in that locale.

In 1973, New York's Governor Rockefeller unveiled his long-awaited proposal for New York's fourth jetport. The site chosen was Stewart Airport, a former Air Force field located 65 miles north of Manhattan on the outskirts of the Hudson River town of Newburgh. Passengers would be moved from the airport to New York's Pennsylvania Station by a 58-minute high-speed rail link, much of it over existing tracks; in addition there would be highways and STOL (short takeoff and landing) planes. The jetport was estimated to cost about $1 billion and by 1990 would be taking care of an estimated 36 million passengers. Not only would it take some of the pressure off the three New York City facilities but would also provide about 29,000 on-site jobs for the Hudson Valley community. But whether the Port Authority, which would build and operate the facility, or the voters of New York State, will ultimately approve the operation remains an open question.

In another problem area, water transportation in the Northeast revolves principally around the coastal traffic and that on the Great Lakes serving Buffalo and Erie. Boston, New York, Philadelphia, and Baltimore are the major ocean-port cities. The commerce they handle is, for the most part, en route to or from other parts of the nation or foreign ports. Portland, Providence, New Haven, and Wilmington are secondary ports, and there are many ports of even less importance.

A few rivers are navigable some distance upstream—the Hudson to Albany, the Delaware to Trenton, and the Connecticut to Hartford. Canals are little used for commerce, except for the New York State Barge Canal, the Cape Cod Canal, and the Chesapeake and Delaware system across the northern end of the Delmarva Peninsula. On the other hand, a great increase in pleasure-boating has meant that some of the nineteenth-century waterways have been rediscovered for recreational use.

THE SEARCH FOR WATER SUPPLIES AND RECREATION AREAS

Increased urbanization and resource use in the Northeast has placed a heavy burden on the fresh-water supplies of the region. Metropolitan centers are reaching out increasingly into rural areas to take care of present and anticipated needs. In the United States, each inhabitant uses an average of 200 gallons of water per year for drinking and another 15,000 gallons for washing, laundry, heating, and waste disposal. In addition, there are demands for water for irrigation (particu-

larly of lawns), recreation, manufacturing, and steam genera-
tion in power plants. All these uses are well developed in the
Northeast.

The region enjoys fairly heavy precipitation throughout the
year. In addition, it has many surface water supplies, such as
lakes Erie, Ontario, and Champlain, and the Finger Lakes of
western New York State. Glacial action has produced a great
number of smaller lakes on which the area may draw for its
needs; unfortunately, most of the major metropolitan centers
(with the exception of Buffalo and Rochester) are located
some distance away from the larger lakes. The Northeast also
has a number of river systems—the Delaware, Susquehanna,
Ohio, Mohawk, and Connecticut—from which fresh water may
be obtained. A problem, however, is that rivers and streams
are frequently used as disposal areas for sewage and industrial
wastes, thus complicating their use for other purposes.

New York City, by far the greatest consumer of water in the
Northeast, has not only tapped water supplies in nearby Westchester and Putnam counties but has constructed reservoirs
in the Catskills and beyond in the upper basin of the Delaware
River, which is over 100 miles from Manhattan Island. A combination of tunnels and aqueducts carries the water to New
York City. The existence of an extensive watershed in a thinly
populated upland region is of great benefit to New York; but
its use of the upper waters of the Delaware River has brought
repercussions from cities downstream on the Delaware, especially Trenton and Philadelphia. In 1931, the Supreme Court
placed limitations on the amount of water New York could take
from the upper Delaware, a restriction that was modified in
New York's favor in 1954, on the condition that New York City
release water from its reservoirs in dry periods in order to
maintain minimum flow in the river.

Problems of water supply in the Delaware Basin led to the
creation, in 1936, of a four-state commission—embracing New
York, New Jersey, Pennsylvania, and Delaware—to coordinate
plans for future use of the river. Known now as the Delaware
River Basin Commission, the organization drew up a Delaware
River Basin Compact, which was adopted in 1961 as joint

legislation by the U.S. government and the four member states. This compact calls for a 50-year development program, at a cost of nearly $600 million, to reduce flood damage, increase water supplies, and provide additional recreational water and hydroelectric power in a 12,765-square-mile area stretching from the Catskills to the mouth of Delaware Bay. For the first time, the focus of all major water-resource activities in the Delaware Basin by the federal government and the separate states is located in a single authority—a move that might well be copied in other river basins, such as those of the Connecticut, the Susquehanna, and the Ohio.

Boston, in its search for water, reaches 60 miles to the west to Quabbin Reservoir; Hartford and Springfield tap watersheds close to one another; while Philadelphia derives its supply from the Delaware and Schuylkill rivers. The latter is also important to the upstream city of Reading. Baltimore needs to go less than 20 miles west for its water supply from three reservoirs, although the city also taps the Susquehanna River 30 miles away. Washington derives its water from the Potomac River, which is upstream from the capital. Pittsburgh also makes use of adjacent river waters, while Buffalo, Rochester, and Erie tap the waters of the Great Lakes.

Western Long Island, with its burgeoning population, is experiencing a slow invasion of salt water, filtering from the Atlantic into the deep sands and gravels that underlie the island. The saline water is advancing eastward across Nassau County at a rate of about 100 feet per year, and wells in the southwestern part of the county have become brackish. Not only has the use of fresh water increased, but not enough water is being returned to the soil. Highways, parking lots, houses, and driveways divert rainwater into streams instead of allowing it to percolate into the ground. Public sewer systems carry waste matter into the sea instead of into septic tanks, from which water can filter into the soil. In July, 1965, New York State authorized the construction of a $4 million nuclear power plant in eastern Long Island that converts sea water into fresh water at a rate of 1 million gallons per day—a possible harbinger of things to come for New York City.

For the urban areas of the Northeast, several factors are important with respect to their future water needs. The first is the need for new watersheds, a need that involves setting aside areas, particularly woodland, for eventual use as reservoir sites. In most of the Northeastern states, voters are asked every election year to approve bond issues to create future reservoirs to serve growing metropolitan needs. As time goes by, the various water-supply systems come closer toward one another, and there is an increasing need for joint planning and legislative action both within and between states of the Northeast.

A second problem is that of pollution. Here, again, greater concentrations of people in metropolitan areas mean greater water-pollution problems and a greater expense in coping with these difficulties. Long-range planning involving many communities is essential in the congested areas of the Northeast. Rivers whose waters are used many times frequently cross state lines, thereby complicating resource-use planning; the example of the interstate agency for the Delaware should be duplicated for a number of other rivers.

There is also the prospect of desalinization, which could provide additional fresh-water supplies for coastal cities. Within the next decade, a major breakthrough may come in the technology of desalinization, and centers like Boston, New York, and Philadelphia may find it more economical to turn to the nearby sea for additional fresh-water needs than to look inland to fulfill their requirements.

Along with water needs are those of recreation; in this respect the Northeast is well suited to urban requirements. To the east of the Boston-Washington corridor are the ocean beaches, stretching from Cape Cod down to Long Island, southward along the Jersey, Delaware, and Maryland shores. One of the problems of this area is that so little of the shorefront along the oceans remains as public property. In addition to salt-water facilities, there are many lakes, ponds, and rivers in this eastern fringe to attract the recreationist, as well as public parks. The Cape Cod National Seashore, Long Island's Jones Beach, and Maryland's Pocomoke State Park are among them.

To the north and west of the Boston-Washington corridor stretch mountains, forests, and lakes to serve the vacationist's needs. The White and Green mountains, the Berkshires and Taconics, the Catskills, the Poconos, and the Catoctins—these and others represent prime vacation spots accessible to the big metropolises. Beyond these are other resorts, such as those in the Adirondacks, the Finger Lakes, and the Alleghenys.

It is true, of course, that many of the residents of the Northeast's metropolitan areas have neither the time nor the money to travel frequently (if indeed at all) to some of the more distant resorts. For them, recreation travel means but a short drive or a bus or subway ride; it is for them, to a large extent, that many of the Green Acres proposals have been directed. Regional planners have long claimed that within or immediately adjacent to large metropolitan areas there should be sizeable districts set aside for public recreation. Such districts, removed from other forms of land use, could be of value for wildlife preservation, for public health, and as public water sites. But because of the expense of acquiring and maintaining such districts, few metropolitan areas of the Northeast have seriously embarked on Green Acres programs. Instead, they continue to rely on public and private parks and recreation areas, many of which are becoming increasingly inadequate for the urban populations.

THE NEED FOR POWER

One of the critical problems facing the Northeast today is the need for inanimate power for electricity, heating, and transportation. Wood is no longer practical as a power source, nor are the many small rapids and waterfalls that once turned the mills. There is coal in Pennsylvania, and small amounts of oil and natural gas there and in southern New York State, but otherwise, there are few natural fuels to supply the expanding power needs. Between 1960 and 1972, electric-energy production in the Northeast doubled. At present, average costs to power companies in the Northeast are higher than anywhere else in the United States, except for the West Coast.

Since the end of World War II, the coal industry has experienced important shifts in its consumer markets. The change of railroads from coal-burning to diesel locomotives, the decreasing use of coal by homeowners, and the expansion of natural-gas pipelines have resulted in a loss of some of the traditional coal markets. But the electric-utility industry in the United States has expanded tremendously, and coal producers have sought to acquire an increasing share in this market. Over 60 percent of the coal produced now goes to electric utilities. In supplying the Northeast with coal, producers have been faced with: 1) the need for reducing the cost of coal to the minehead through more efficient mining; 2) the high cost of transporting coal; and 3) competition from other power sources for the market. Many of the older coal mines are in Pennsylvania. Production here has been curtailed to the point that the state's coal output is now less than half of what it was immediately after World War II. West Virginia's production, however, has declined considerably less, and much of the coal used by New York and New England is from West Virginia.

In order to reduce transportation costs, some companies have located power plants at the mines and move the electricity out through transmission lines; but the problem with this is the expense of maintaining such lines and the considerable loss of power that occurs in transporting it over long distances. A second method of reducing costs is to mix powdered coal with water and pump the coal slurry from the mines directly to the utility plants—a process already in operation in Ohio between Cadiz and Cleveland. But the traditional movement of coal is still by rail.

All along the eastern coast are cities receiving fuel oil and gasoline by tanker; for many ports, such as Providence and New Haven, petroleum products make up 80 to 90 percent of the imports handled by the harbor. From here, the fuel may be sent inland by pipeline or truck. In addition, pipelines from the great mid-continental field bring oil and natural gas directly to the Northeast for use not only in heating and transportation but also—occurring more frequently now—in the electric power industry. Because of the well-developed transport facilities, the Northeast has good access to supplies of the three major fossil fuels—coal, petroleum, and natural gas.

Other power sources are also being developed: hydroelectric, nuclear, and tidal. While there are few large hydroelectric installations on the rivers of the Northeast, considerable development has been taking place at Niagara Falls and on the St. Lawrence River bordering New York State. By 1972, New York's installed, generating hydroelectric capacity was the fourth greatest in the nation, after Washington, California, and Oregon. The surplus power available from the Niagara Falls and St. Lawrence plants is fed into a statewide grid for distribution in power-deficient areas.

Another potential source of hydroelectric power is the proposed Dickey-Lincoln Dam on St. John's River in northern Maine. Slated to cost at least a half billion dollars, the two-mile-long, earth-filled dam would back up the St. John's and its tributaries for over 50 miles and would flood nearly 90,000 acres of forest with an artificial lake. Environmentalists and sportsmen's groups are bitterly opposed to the destruction of one of the last remaining wildlife areas in the eastern United States. Proponents of the plan point to the Northeast's need for power, to the potential economic gains for some of the more economically depressed areas of New England, and to the fact that most of the area that would be under water is cut-over timberland.

Another power source may be offshore oil. While seabed areas on George's Bank off New England and Baltimore Canyon off New Jersey and Delaware have yet to be put up for lease, there appear to be good prospects of commercially recoverable reserves both of oil and natural gas being located in these areas. These resources would presumably be moved to adjacent land areas, there to be refined and made available to Northeastern communities. But several issues are involved here. One is the opposition of environmentalist and other groups that remember the Santa Barbara oil spill and are concerned about the prospect of fouling the coastlines of Maine, Cape Cod, Long Island, and the Jersey shore. What assurances do they have that such accidents will not take place on the Atlantic shelf? Other groups are afraid that picturesque recreation areas such as the Isle of Shoals, Chatham, Massachusetts, and eastern Long Island will in time be used as staging areas for oil operations and come to resemble Morgan City, Louisiana, or Aberdeen, Scotland. Then there is the time element. Oil company officials suggest a lapse of up to eight years between the time when a decision is made to bid on an offshore lease and when commerical production is underway. So no matter what transpires over the next few years with regard to offshore leasing and exploratory work, it will probably be the mid-1980s at the earliest before the Northeast derives much benefit from energy produced from offshore resources.

The first nuclear power plant in the nation was opened in December of 1957 at Shippingport, Pennsylvania, on the Ohio River downstream from Pittsburgh. This was followed by two other plants, one at Rowe in northwestern Massachusetts and the other at Buchanan in Westchester County, about 30 miles north of New York City. By 1974, there were twenty-two nuclear power plants in operation in the Northeast, with twenty-two more scheduled for completion by 1983. Rhode Island was the only state without a nuclear plant either in operation or in the planning stage. Nuclear plants in New England alone supplied over 20 percent of the area's energy in 1974, compared with a national average of 7 percent. But even this rate is seen by power forecasters as inadequate to meet regional needs, particularly in the light of impending oil shortages. Between 1970 and 1985, the domestic consumption of electricity is expected to double in the United States. Power companies estimate a time lag of ten years between the inauguration of plans to build a nuclear power plant at a particular site and its coming into full production. Many of the sites initially sought have to be abandoned due to opposition from environmental groups or local residents, or as a result of unfavorable environmental test results. Not only might the Northeast as a unit become increasingly a net importer of energy, but the urbanized Boston-Washington corridor could before long experience an acute energy crisis and thus look to Maine, western New York State, and western Pennsylvania to increase their production of nuclear and other forms of power in order to alleviate the situation along the seaboard.

A final power source for the Northeast is in the tides. In July, 1963, President Kennedy initiated action on a program to harness the tides in Passamaquoddy Bay, on the Maine-New Brunswick border, to provide electric power, which will be shared by the U.S. and Canada. This bay is an arm of the Bay of Fundy, which has a rise and fall of tides amounting to over 25 feet. At high tide, gates will be opened, permitting the filling of a large pool. The waters of the pool will then be dropped through turbines into a low pool that, when filled, will be drained back into the Bay of Fundy during low tide. But the chances for the development of the Passamaquoddy site seem to grow dimmer with the passage of time.

THE POLITICAL IMPACT OF POPULATION SHIFTS

Throughout the Northeast, a traditional political pattern has existed during past decades: the cities tend to be largely Democratic, and the rural areas and small towns largely Republican. This pattern has been true particularly in presidential and congressional elections and in elections of state senators and representatives. It is less true with respect to governors and local officials. Coupled with this pattern is another—that of voting districts for congressional representatives and state representatives. These districts are determined by the respective state legislatures, and over the years, the rural-dominated legislatures have devised formulas that deny the urban entities the representation they merit on the basis of population. This situation has, of course, been further complicated by the growth of the suburbs, where underrepresentation has existed.

Let us first take the case of congressional representation. Because of population changes between 1960 and 1970, the Northeast suffered a net loss of four seats in the House of Representatives. Pennsylvania and New York each lost two representatives; the other states neither gained nor lost. This trend has existed for some time. In the four decades of 1930 to 1970, the Northeast suffered a net loss of fifteen seats in the House. Pennsylvania alone lost nine; New York, six; Massachusetts, three; and Maine, one; while New Jersey gained one, and Maryland gained three.

Also important is the pattern of congressional districts within the separate states. In the early 1960s there was considerable disparity among districts. Although on a national average there was at that time a member of the House of Representatives for each 410,000 people, Maryland's Fifth District—which includes the suburbs east of Washington—had a 1960 population of 711,000, while the First District, embracing the eastern shore, had a population of only 244,000. In Connecticut, the First District (covering Hartford and the northern Connecticut River Valley) had 690,000 people, but the Fifth District in the northwestern part of the state had only 319,000.

In 1963, and again early in 1964, the Supreme Court of the United States ruled that unequal apportionment deprived citizens of equal protection under the law as guaranteed by the Fourteenth Amendment. This ruling held that: "One man's vote in a congressional election must be worth as much as another's." State legislatures subsequently began redrawing the boundaries of congressional districts, thereby redressing the imbalance that has tended to give rural voters such a disproportionate share in congressional representation.

In June of 1964, the Supreme Court ruled again; this time with respect to uneven apportionment in both houses of the state legislatures. This action was based on a 1962 ruling that federal courts have authority to review state legislature apportionments that are subjected to legal challenge; the Court's 1964 decision "requires that the seats in both houses of a bicameral state legislature be apportioned on a population basis." Action was to be taken by the states by 1966, and the lower courts could prohibit elections if apportionment were found to be unconstitutional. Reapportionment in the individual states was to be carried out at least once every ten years thereafter, in order to conform with future population shifts.

In Maine, New Hampshire, and Vermont, the Republicans generally dominate both houses of the state legislature; while in Massachusetts, Rhode Island, and Maryland, the Democrats are more often in control. Rhode Island has traditionally sent only Democrats to Congress, and Vermont only Republicans. But Vermont, New Hampshire, and Maine have, in recent years, all elected Democratic governors, and Rhode Island elected a Republican. This indicates a gradual breakdown in solid-party states in this region, and a tendency for the Northeast to participate in national political swings—for example, favoring Johnson in 1964 and Nixon in 1972 and voting against the Republicans in 1974.

THE RISE OF TECHNOLOGICAL UNEMPLOYMENT

In the discussions of the preceding sections it has been, of course, impossible to always differentiate between the processes of urbanization and those of technology, insofar as they are causative factors in the changing landscape of the Northeast. For example, urbanization has meant new transportation needs; so, too, has technology, which contributes to the obsolescence of the street railways, the intercoastal passenger ships, and the ferry boats. Consider also the role of technology in highway construction through and around cities, in sewage treatment plants, and in the development of high-rise apartments. To this list we now add an additional economic factor—the impact on the Northeast of unemployment resulting from technological change.

New England and the Middle Atlantic area were the first in the U.S. to experience the effects of the Industrial Revolution. There were few mineral or power resources, except for waterpower and coal; but as industrialization grew, the area came to acquire a large reservoir of unskilled and semiskilled labor. This labor was utilized in mining, lumbering, shipping, trade, and the manufacture of such products as textiles, shoes, machinery and processed foods. All these fields expanded during the nineteenth and early twentieth centuries; by the outbreak of World War I, however, some of them began to decline. This decline has continued at varying rates during the past fifty years in all these fields, except in retail trade; and other fields, such as agriculture and quarrying, have also experienced continuous downward trends. In their place has come an expansion of tertiary industries such as tourism, finance, education, and government work.

Consider, for example, the case of coal. In 1948, coal accounted for 45 percent of energy fuels consumed; by 1973 the figure had dropped to 19 percent. The average daily output of coal per miner more than doubled during this same period because of improved mining techniques and the use of machinery, with the result that the number of persons employed in coal-mining has dropped substantially. This is particularly true in the case of anthracite-mining. The total U.S. supply comes from Pennsylvania, where fewer than 6,000 persons are now employed in the industry. Or consider the case of textiles: in New England alone, the number of workers dropped from 450,000 at the end of World War I to 280,000 in 1947, to less than 80,000 by 1973. In shoes and leather, paper, metals, and other products the Northeast continues to witness a decline in employment. This results from changed market demands, obsolescent plants, and competition from manufacturing in other parts of the nation.

There is something of a spiralling effect to the unemployment and underemployment picture in the Northeast. The past two decades have witnessed an out-migration of persons in the 18–45 age group who are in search of better opportunities, leaving behind a high proportion of the aged, children, and people who are physically and mentally disabled. Concomitant effects are a rise in the number of persons on relief rolls and an increase in funds for state public assistance. Such conditions exist not only among the ghettos of the big cities but also in more extensive geographic areas, such as Providence-Pawtucket, Fall River-New Bedford; Manchester, New Hampshire; Rome-Utica; Reading, Pennsylvania; and Paterson, New Jersey. It holds true for the hard- and soft-coal mining regions of Pennsylvania, the quarrying towns of northern New England, and the farming areas of most of the Northeast. It also pertains to sectors of the larger cities, where industries and the skilled workers have moved out, leaving behind a disproportionate number of unskilled and underemployed. High tax rates (caused, in part, by the rising cost of services) coupled with labor demands (brought on, in part, by anxiety over future employment) have led many industries in the Northeast to relocate to other parts of the nation, leaving behind blighted areas, unemployment, and increased relief needs. Yet these conditions exist at a time when parts of the Northeast are dazzling with new bridges, jetports, superhighways, skyscraper developments, and an ever-increasing pattern of middle- and upper-income suburbs. Poverty in the midst of plenty is the paradox of the Northeast.

Inflation coupled with recession has placed tremendous pressure on urban budgets all over the U.S. This is particularly true in areas of the Northeast where many cities are already in financial straits. In 1974, New York City was predicting a cost rise of $280 million over the anticipated budget and a revenue shortage of $150 million. Part of the deficit might have been made up by firing 15,000 city employees, instituting a 100 percent freeze on hiring, and by selling off some city properties (see page 72). Baltimore imposed a freeze on civil service hiring such that only replacements were permitted. In Boston, a major share of the city's income comes from real estate taxes, but the city's budget was in jeopardy because of the fact that 60 percent of the property in the city was (and is) tax exempt and because half of the daily work force lives in the suburbs and thus contributes nothing to the city's upkeep.

INCREASED PRESSURES ON THE COASTAL ZONE

Of the eleven Northeastern states, nine border on the North Atlantic Ocean. Pennsylvania and the District of Columbia have access through estuaries that are open to navigation; in addition, Pennsylvania and New York border on the Great Lakes, which are often considered part of the nation's marine environment. In the Northeast, only Vermont is landlocked.

The length of shoreline of the Northeast (see Table 2) is 14 percent of the U.S. total, but along the coast are many opportunities for access to the sea/bays, estuaries, natural harbors, sandy beaches and offshore islands, rivers, creeks, and tidal

TABLE 2. The length of the shoreline of the Northeast

State	Tidal shoreline (statute miles)
Maine	3,478
New Hampshire	131
Massachusetts	1,519
Rhode Island	384
Connecticut	618
New York	1,850
New Jersey	1,792
Pennsylvania	89
Delaware	381
Maryland	3,190
Total	12,432

inlets. Moreover, most of the upland areas adjacent to the coast consist of gently rolling to moderate terrain, permitting settlement and use on or close to the coast. In the offshore waters are valuable fishing resources, along with anticipated oil and gas reserves on the generally broad continental shelf.

The term "coastal zone" is a functional one, describing a strip along the coast consisting both of the land area adjacent to the shore and the immediate offshore waters. Both landward and seaward boundaries are flexible, depending in part on the purposes for which the coastal-zone concept is intended. The 1972 Coastal Zone Management Act describes the coastal zone as extending "inland from the shoreline only to the extent necessary to control shorelands, the use of which have a direct and significant impact on the coastal waters." The act leaves it to the individual states to set the precise landward limits of the zone for management purposes. Some definitions use the criterion of contours above sea level; others, a specific distance inland from the shore. Since the coastal zone is a functional area, the definition of its limits should relate to the functions it serves.

There are a variety of uses to which the coastal zone may be put. Among these are: 1) recreational and residential; 2) commercial and industrial; 3) military and other institutional; and 4) conservation. There are many alternative uses within these categories. Recreation, for example, may be either public or private in nature and ranges from New York's Coney Island to the private summer estates of Bar Harbor, Maine. Residential use may involve single-family dwellings or high-rise condominiums. In general, recreational and residential uses are expensive because they tend to preclude other uses, particularly those associated with environmental pollution.

There may be other forms of use in conflict in the coastal zone; for example, waste disposal and shellfishing, commercial and sports fishing, and private property rights and public access to the shoreline. In an area both as affluent and as congested as many parts of the Northeast, these conflicts are often intense, and their resolution involves both expense and jurisdictional accommodations. With respect to the latter, the individual states own the offshore areas to three nautical miles out from shore; beyond this are ocean areas under federal ownership. In some parts of the Northeast, as between Maine and New Hampshire, the coastal states themselves are involved in jurisdictional problems. Even leaving boundary-delimitation issues aside, it is clear that what one state does in its offshore waters (as, for example, in Long Island Sound) may seriously impinge on the interests of a neighboring state. And when it comes to bays, tidal ponds, river mouths, and other coastal irregularities, the state may or may not vest all or some forms of jurisdiction to individual townships, counties, or cities, thereby further complicating juridical issues. As a final note, the Army Corps of Engineers has certain rights within the navigable waters of the U.S., a term that includes the U.S. territorial sea to three miles from shore.

The "urge to the sea" in the Northeast may be seen in a number of forms. Over the past several decades, for example, there have been great increases in population in a number of coastal counties. Among these are Rockingham County, New Hampshire; Barnstable County, Massachusetts; Suffolk

County, Long Island; and Monmouth and Ocean counties, New Jersey. There is the establishment of national seashores on Cape Cod, Assateague Island, and—in the near future— New York Harbor. There is the phenomenal rise in land costs along or in sight of the shore; the pressure for siting nuclear power plants along the coast; the improvement of highway and bridge connections to and along the coast; the growth of marinas, pleasure boats, sports fishing, and scuba diving; and, last but not least, the pressures by environmental groups to protect and preserve the marine environment of the Northeast. One focus of the struggle has been the wetlands, which provide sanctuaries for wildlife, nursery grounds for commercial fish stocks, and potential building sites for developers.

A key to coastal zone use is effective management—a process that involves federal, state, and local levels of government in a highly complex system. The 1972 Coastal Zone Management Act vests the primary responsibility for management with the states; they, in turn, may set up the appropriate machinery to carry out management responsibilities, with financial and other forms of assistance from Washington. Both New York and Massachusetts, for example, have initiated comprehensive planning for their coastal areas. One of the most active groups has been the Nassau-Suffolk Regional Planning Board of Long Island, and another the Massachusetts Commission on Ocean Management. Maine has prepared a Penobscot Bay Resource Plan, which provides a detailed inventory of natural resources and existing and potential uses of the coastal area. Rhode Island has a full-fledged Coastal Zone Council with legal power to issue permits based on a comprehensive statewide plan for coastal zone use. Such activities are indicative of the growing awareness within and among coastal states of the need to protect and wisely utilize their coastal areas and resources. This need will become even more apparent once large-scale oil and gas exploration and exploitation begins on Georges' Bank and in the Baltimore Canyon area.

Still another facet of coastal zone management and use involves the projected extension of national control over ocean resources out to 200 miles from shore. This will affect commercial fisheries (the resources of the seabed and subsoil on the shelf are already within U.S. jurisdiction) and should also lead to considerably expanded fishing activities in the Northeast. But it may also involve management of the marginal waters themselves, including environmental protection, greater control over shipping activities beyond territorial limits, and an increased interest in the resources of the shelf. State boundaries may in time be extended seaward (particularly if and when the U.S. goes to a twelve-mile territorial sea), and there may be greater interest in other uses of the seabed (as for recreation, storage sites, and so on) and the waters themselves (as for offshore power sites). These facets of coastal zone management support the view that a new geographic unit—the coastal margin, or belt, combining both the coastal zone and the offshore areas out to perhaps 200 miles — will before long emerge as a distinct management entity.

3 The Urban Axis

The urbanized northeastern seaboard of the U.S. is a unique geographic phenomenon. It is unique in the size of its population, in the extent of its urbanized areas, in the wealth it engenders, and in its role not only with respect to the rest of the nation but also to the entire globe. Here are located several of the world's major seaports, its greatest financial center, and a number of its major educational and research institutions. Here also is an area where the value added by manufactures is greater than that for almost any nation of the world. This is the primary region of the United States in retail and wholesale trade, in printing and publishing, in the arts, and of course, in government activities.

In his study of the northeastern seaboard, Gottmann terms "the unique cluster of metropolitan areas" to be found in this region a "Megalopolis." He refers to it as "the continent's economic hinge" because of the role played by port cities in determining whether the nation's economic door would be opened to world trade or closed in order to concentrate on internal economic development. "They alone in the country had enough capital, skill, and authority to elaborate such policies and profit by their applications." These ports were at first on the edge of the inland wilderness. Later, because of roads, canals, and railroads, they were able to tap the riches of the developing Midwest and to serve its growing population. The Northeast itself became the first industrialized area of the United States, and here again, the port cities benefited from the imports and exports. Finally, the region worked hard to become the financial, commercial, and cultural center of the nation. The changing roles these cities have played since the start of the twentieth century form one of the dominant themes in any regional analysis of the Northeast.

According to a *Fortune* magazine survey in 1972, the following were located in Megalopolis: 40 percent of the 500 largest industrial corporation headquarters; 40 percent of the nation's 50 largest utilities; one-half of the 50 largest life insurance companies (including 14 of the top 15); one-half of the 50 largest retailing firms; one-third of the 50 largest commercial banks; one-quarter of the 50 largest transportation companies. Here, also, are 13 of the 50 largest urban areas.

In this chapter, we shall consider the urbanized Boston-Washington axis as divided into the four subregions noted on page 15: southern New England, Metropolitan New York, the Delaware Valley, and the Baltimore-Washington conurbation. While the borders between these subdivisions are often not clearly defined, each one has certain characteristics of its own, and each should be considered as a separate unit within the overall framework of the urban axis. While all four of the units face the common problems enumerated in Chapter 2, they have at times adopted differing methods of dealing with them. Also, it must be remembered that economic and social trends in these four subregions are by no means similar. As a result, they face different problems of adjustment to changing conditions.

SOUTHERN NEW ENGLAND

The urbanized axis of southern New England starts in the east with the Greater Boston area, extends west through Worcester and Springfield, runs down the Connecticut Valley past Hartford, and then moves southwest through New Haven and Bridgeport, linking with the New York region. An offshoot from Boston would extend south to include the cities of Providence, Fall River, and New Bedford.

This is one of the oldest industrial areas in the nation. Even before the Civil War the cotton mills were well established and utilized waterpower, a plentiful labor supply from either immigration or small towns and farms, and the available investment capital. For many decades, southeastern New England led the United States in cotton and wool manufactures and in the production of shoes and leather. The metals industry also developed, particularly in Connecticut and western Massachusetts. For a long time Boston was second only to New York as a national port. Not until World War I was its total value of exports and imports exceeded by Philadelphia and Baltimore. From an early dominance in industry and commerce, southern New England (particularly after World War I) suffered a gradual decline in its traditional economy and subsequently developed a need for reallocation of its resources.

The Greater Boston area consists of a series of semicircles about the city itself. The first, immediately adjacent to Boston, includes such industrial cities as Cambridge, Somerville, and Watertown; beyond these are Lynn, Salem, Waltham, and Quincy. Farther out are Haverhill, Lawrence, Lowell, and Brockton. Finally, there is the outermost semicircle—Fitchburg, Worcester, Woonsocket, and Providence. Serving these various cities is a radial network of railroads and highways, emanating from Boston. Many smaller towns lie between Boston and the peripheral cities; but there is also considerable open space into which the suburbs are expanding.

The port of Boston stands eighth in the nation in volume of imports, but seventeenth in exports. Boston's harbor is open throughout the year and is closer to northwestern Europe than are those of New York, Philadelphia, and Baltimore. Its major imports are petroleum, foodstuffs, and raw wool for the surrounding textile plants. The port's growth in recent years has failed to keep pace with that of New York, Philadelphia, and Baltimore, due in part to its limited trade hinterland. But there are also troubles within Boston itself, including labor problems, a high pilferage rate, and outmoded port facilities scattered over miles of waterfront. In recent years, the Massachusetts Port Authority (Massport), which also operates Logan International Airport, opened a $25 million Moran Terminal designed to take care of the harbor's requirements. But Boston already needs a larger public terminal and an offshore oil complex. The port's future seems to lie primarily in oil and containerization, the latter being particularly well adapted to southeastern New England's export trade.

Among the dominant industries in southeastern New England are textiles, leather goods, machinery (particularly electrical), and wearing apparel. There is also a great variety of other types of manufactures, such as jewelry, metals, shipbuilding, abrasives, paper products, rubber goods, and chemicals. Such variety lends stability to the economic structure, for if one branch of manufacturing is down, others may still be in strong positions.

The cotton-textile industry was concentrated largely in southeastern Massachusetts and Rhode Island; it reached its peak in New England just prior to World War I when there were over 18 million active cotton spindles. But the last cotton-weaving mill left Rhode Island in 1968, and most of the mills in the Greater Boston area are gone also. In some instances, they have relocated to the state of Maine, where labor costs are cheaper, but for the most part they have moved to other parts of the United States.

The woolen mills are largely located in the Merrimack Valley cities, north of Boston, as well as in northern Rhode Island. The decline has been less severe in this area than in the cotton trade. Leather goods are another traditional industry of southeastern New England, particularly in Boston, Brockton, Haverhill, and Lynn. Availability of skilled labor was a significant factor in this industry's location; but in recent decades proximity to markets and raw materials has become increasingly important, and much of the industry has moved to the Middle West and the Southeast. Another of the older industries is the wearing apparel industry, including underwear, shirts, and blouses. In this industry, eastern New England has done relatively well in retaining the business, although automation has somewhat decreased the employment opportunities.

The Boston area is important for machinery, including textile and shoe machines, electrical products, and machine parts and tools. There are over 500 electrical-machinery plants in the Boston area alone. Many of them are located along Route 128, the "electronics highway," where the research facilities of Harvard and M.I.T. contribute to the heavy concentration. It should be noted that much of the electronics industry is geared toward U.S. government needs; and the government can be a capricious customer—there are the possibilities of reductions, particularly in Defense Department spending, and of competition from other regions of the United States for research and development contracts.

"It's nice to live there if you can afford it." This statement may be heard over and over again in reference to southeastern New England. There are plenty of city slums and run-down mill towns; but there are also delightful villages, pleasant towns, and charming parts of the larger cities. The proximity of seashore, mountains, and other cities and towns is one of the area's greatest assets. Unfortunately, its economy is not as strong as that of the New York-Washington area, and there is considerable unemployment or employment with wages and opportunities less than those of other parts of the nation.

Traditionally, the federal government has been important here, in both defense contracts and through military expenditures. But, as noted earlier, southeastern New England is in the process of losing important bases. The April, 1974, decision by the Department of Defense to close or curtail over 250 military bases seriously affected Boston and Rhode Island. The Boston Navy Yard is to be closed, thereby eliminating 5,200 jobs. Otis Air Base on Cape Cod is also to be phased out. In Rhode Island there will be an 80 percent cut in the military payroll. Closure of the Quonset Point Naval Air Station and the Davisville Seabee Base means that over 4,000 civilian jobs will be lost, along with an equal number of military positions. The departure of the military will have a strong, adverse effect on the life of the towns where these families lived. The Newport Naval Base is scheduled to be shut down, eliminating 725 civilian jobs and moving over 13,000 military personnel and their families to other East Coast areas. The Atlantic Cruiser-Destroyer Fleet and other naval vessels are to be sent to Norfolk, Virginia; Charleston, South Carolina; and Mayport, Florida. The only potential gain to southeastern New England by these actions is the release of some of the government-held land and buildings for use by the state and local towns. One substitute employer for Quonset Point is the Electric Boat Company of Groton, Connecticut. This company already employs several thousand Rhode Islanders at Groton in the manufacture of submarines; it now plans to utilize some of the former military land in Rhode Island for expanded production of submarine parts.

Although the Boston area is still the eighth largest industrial center in North America, it continues to suffer from a lack of industrial growth. About two-thirds of the jobs in the metropolitan area employ people in the trade, service, and government fields. The incomes of many of the families, while not at the poverty level, are low enough to cause hardships, particularly at times of inflation. Perhaps this is one of the reasons why residents of the South Boston-Roxbury area reacted so violently, in the fall of 1974, to court-ordered school busing in racially imbalanced school districts. The fury of many whites may to some extent reflect their frustration at the lack of economic progress in this predominantly middle-income area.

Southwestern New England differs somewhat from southeastern New England—first, in the absence of a metropolitan hub, and second, in the relatively few textile, shoe, and leather plants. Machinery, tools, and instruments are significant industries, along with aircraft, brass, and typewriters. Because of these activities, the region, in the past few decades, has not suffered from as great economic difficulties as has southeastern New England.

The largest industry in southwestern New England is United Aircraft of Hartford, which owns such companies as Pratt and Whitney of West Hartford and Sikorsky Aircraft of Stratford.

Waterbury, in the Naugatuck River Valley, is one of the nation's brass centers; New Britain is a hardware center; while nearby Meriden is the home of International Silver. Ball bearings are produced in Bristol and New Britain, and typewriters in Hartford.

Services are also important. Hartford has long been an insurance city, while New Haven, in addition to its manufacturing activities, is also an educational and research center. With their hills and lakes, western Connecticut and Massachusetts have for decades been centers for summer vacationists; now winter vacationists flock there from nearby urban areas, and the region is dotted with winter sports facilities. In addition, southwestern Connecticut is becoming more and more of a residential area for New York City.

Like the Greater Boston area, much of southwestern New England is a mixture of old and new industries. Despite the movement away of much of the national market, the forces of tradition may have kept much of the brass, hardware, typewriter, and machine industries in the region. Here are factories specializing in light manufacturing, which requires few raw materials or power but requires advanced mechanical skills. Their products have small bulk and can withstand transport charges to distant markets. Even the aircraft plants do not generally handle the assembly of finished products but specialize in machine parts. In the coming years, southwestern New England stands to benefit from its proximity to New York City, out of which industries and people are constantly moving in ever-widening circles.

METROPOLITAN NEW YORK

The area entitled Metropolitan New York is one of the major manufacturing regions of the United States, specializing in clothing, printing and publishing, chemicals, food processing, machinery, and a wide variety of other items. Here, also, is the world's greatest port, its foremost financial center, and the home of many of the nation's leading businesses.

The city of New York consists of five boroughs—Manhattan,

the Bronx, Brooklyn, Queens, and Richmond. Within the city, manufacturing employs about 600,000 people, some one-quarter of whom are in apparel and related products. Printing and publishing enterprises account for nearly 100,000 employees, followed by food processing. In all, over 10 percent of the nation's factory output is New York based.

Two phenomena are important in manufacturing in New York City. The first is the large number of manufacturing establishments, which comprise close to one-eighth of the nation's total. Many of these small enterprises are able to exploit the supply of low-cost—particularly black—labor. Second, the number of people engaged in manufacturing has been declining. From a peak of just over 1 million in the early 1950s, there has been a steady drop of close to 400,000 between 1953 and 1973. Much of this time, the losses in manufacturing were more than made up for by increases in the availability of office work, services, and government jobs. Since 1969, however, this has not been true, and nearly 200,000 jobs have been lost by the city—many of them to the surrounding communities, where it is easier and cheaper to produce goods. A great many of the jobs lost were among the poorer paying positions, which employed women, blacks, and Puerto Ricans. A recent survey showed an unemployment rate in the South Bronx of 17 percent, rising to 40 percent among the 18- to 22-year-old age group. Of the families in central and east Harlem, over 25 percent were on welfare in 1970 to 1971, a figure that has risen somewhat since then. The corresponding figure for the South Bronx was nearly 40 percent.

The port of New York handles about 40 percent of the value of American foreign trade, or four times that of its nearest rival, New Orleans, Louisiana. New York's magnificent harbor attracted shipping early, and the opening of the Erie Canal in 1825 gave the city a head start over its East Coast rivals for commerce from and to the Midwest. The port has extensive wharves, warehouses, and other terminal facilities and is served by ten major trunk railroads and six short lines. Within five hours of trucking time live nearly 50 million people. New York's 25,000 longshoremen provide highly skilled service, although the city has been plagued by strikes and work stoppages.

New York is predominantly a general cargo port specializing in high-value package shipments. It contains the first free trade zone in the United States (a zone through which cargoes moving from one foreign country to another or must pass or to which goods come to be processed before clearance through customs). The city's hinterland, which extends west to Chicago and southwest to the Ohio River, is hotly contested by other ports such as Baltimore, Philadelphia, and New Orleans. New York must rely on its concentration of shipping facilities, the speed of dispatch of cargoes through the city, and its large internal market capacity in order to maintain its commercial dominance in coming years. One way to insure this dominance is through the construction of new facilities, particularly for containerized cargoes. In late 1974, New York City and the Port Authority of New York and New Jersey agreed to construct a modern containership port in the Red Hook section of Brooklyn. Other terminals are being constructed or improved in Elizabeth, Newark, and Hoboken, New Jersey, on Manhattan Island, and along the Brooklyn waterfront. Over the past several years public and private investment in waterfront facilities has totalled nearly $500 million. Nearly one-fifth of this has gone into the modernization of the Brooklyn Port Authority Marine Terminal, which extends two miles south of the Brooklyn Bridge. A five-year, $76 million project is underway to quadruple the capacity of the Northeast Marine Terminal, New York's first container port; while in New Jersey, the $250 million Elizabeth Marine Terminal—the world's first and largest container port—is being expanded. A $40 million sugar refinery is under construction on Staten Island. In the Bronx stands a refrigerated warehouse that may ultimately handle about two-thirds of the nation's meat imports. Although fewer ships now enter the harbor, those that do tend to be larger. In both tonnage of cargo handled and import duties, New York has experienced increases over the past several years.

New York is the terminus of most of the nation's transatlantic lines, as well as of many of its cruise ships. But transatlantic traffic has been dropping sharply due to competition from air travel. In 1974, the liner the *S. S. France* ended its transatlantic service. Its disappearance from New York cost the port an estimated $150 million annual contribution, including $750,000 in longshoremen's wages. A few months after the *France* terminated its New York service, the city opened its $40 million passenger terminal on the Hudson River. The terminal, which took twenty years to plan, contains berths for six ocean liners, a 1,700-foot-long road system, and air-conditioned, three-level piers, with telescoping gangways similar to those used at airports. But an open question is whether or not the new terminal can reverse the downward trend in ocean-going passenger liners utilizing New York. In the early 1960s, over a million persons sailed in and out of the port; a decade later, the number had dropped to just over 600,000 (compared with close to 12 million overseas travelers utilizing New York's three jetports). Even the cruise business has been cut into by the fly-sail vacation package tours that enable passengers to fly to Miami, or some other warm-water port, and from there embark on cruises.

One advantage New York has enjoyed over other United States cities is the existence of its Port Authority of New York and New Jersey. Founded in 1921, the Authority has jurisdiction over transportation facilities within a 25-mile radius of lower Manhattan Island. Among its nearly $4 billion worth of holdings are the three New York airports, the George Washington Bridge, the Lincoln and Holland tunnels, the new skyscraper World Trade Center, and a number of marine terminals in the Greater New York area. Despite its history of success, the Port Authority has recently experienced financial difficulties, due in part to a drop in use of the airports, tunnels, and bridges. The George Washington Bridge and the Lincoln and Holland Tunnels, for example, have been consistent money-makers for the Authority. Moreover, it has become embroiled in a controversy between New York and New Jersey concerning new rapid transit lines. New York wants the Authority to undertake construction of a rail link from Kennedy

Airport to Manhattan. As part of a *quid pro quo,* New Jersey is seeking a rapid transit line from Newark's railroad station to the Newark International Airport and 15 miles beyond to serve communities as far away as Plainfield. New Jersey also favors a trackage connection in the Jersey Meadows to bring Erie-Lackawanna commuter trains directly into Manhattan. All told, the costs of these three major projects might approach $1 billion—a sizeable amount, even with federal assistance, for an agency already in financial difficulty.

One hopeful sign for New York is the pending establishment of a Gateway National Recreation Area in the Lower New York Bay area. The 20,000-acre unit would be composed of Breezy Point Park and islands in Jamaica Bay, Queens; Sandy Hook State Park, New Jersey; Great Kills Park on the eastern shore of Staten Island; and Hoffman and Swinburne islands, between Brooklyn and Staten Island, at the entrance to New York Harbor. The sites would be connected by low-fare ferries, and the project, if adequately funded, could provide much-needed public marine recreational facilities for the Greater New York area.

The city's commercial position is also evident with regard to air transportation. Forty international and domestic airlines utilize the three major air terminals. The problem of air congestion is particularly acute on weekends and holidays, and air-holding patterns must take into account air traffic using the Philadelphia and southern New England airports.

In terms of services, New York is unparalleled in the United States. It is the advertising center of the nation and the headquarters for one-quarter of the country's 500 largest industrial corporations. One-seventh of the wholesale trade transactions in the United States are made here, while New York's $16 billion per year consumer market accounts for the tremendous volume of retail trade carried on in the city

The factor of concentration is significant here, both for manufacturing and for the service industries. While location and harbor site were important for the city's initial impetus —and rail, highway, and air transportation links have tended to enhance New York's position—it is the continual focusing of activities and people in the New York area that has served as a magnet, drawing in a still greater range of activities. The expansion of New York as an industrial, commercial, financial, educational, and cultural center has been matched by similar growth throughout the rest of the nation. Indeed, in some respects New York has declined in relation to the rest of the United States. But with the exception of manufacturing, its activities continue to grow substantially. It attracts thousands of new residents each year, and the problems of housing, transportation, and public facilities become increasingly difficult for authorities to handle on the municipal, state, and federal levels.

To some experts, New York appears to have become too large, and they favor trends toward decentralization of activities. Such decentralization might be directed away from New York City itself into nearby areas or completely away into other parts of the nation. But in a free economy, the benefits of such policies must be demonstrated to decision-makers in the private economy sector. Although some evidence of decentralizing action exists, it tends to be offset by the attraction to New York of management, advertising, research, the arts, and finance. Lincoln Center, the Chase Manhattan Tower, the Pan Am Building, and the World Trade Center are not designed to serve only the city itself; rather, they have been planned as attractions to New York for various types of activities from other areas—an obvious refutation of decentralizing schemes.

To the east of New York City, population and industry have moved to Long Island. Between 1950 and 1960 Nassau County, east of Queens, nearly doubled in population; while Suffolk County, occupying the easternmost part of Long Island, grew by one and a half times. But during the next decade, while Suffolk County maintained a healthy 68 percent growth rate in population, Nassau County increased by only 9 percent—a figure below that of the national average. There are no large urban areas on Long Island east of Brooklyn and Queens. The 2.6 million people there are sprawled out in towns and suburbs. Industry has also expanded; among those that have settled on Long Island are aviation (Republic and Grumman), electronics (Sperry), and publishing (Doubleday).

Farming is an important activity, particularly in Suffolk County, where ducks, potatoes, and fresh vegetables are leading commodities. The remarkable thing about Long Island is that despite its large population, there is a noticeable lack of settlement and industrial concentration and a noticeable amount of almost continuous scattering. Furthermore, Long Island is, with regard to transportation, a dead-end street. Only in the New York City area is it possible to drive off the Island to the mainland. It is interesting to speculate on the effects of the proposed Orient Point-Connecticut bridge on the area: Long Island, with its substantial areas of empty land, would then become a transit route between southeastern New England and New York City.

North of New York, population and industry have also expanded, but not in the same way as on Long Island. For one thing, the land is more hilly here than in Nassau and Suffolk counties; for another, there is a longer history of urban settlement and land use. Westchester and Putnam counties, lying between the Connecticut line and the Hudson, are traditional areas of wealthy estates, parks and reservoirs, golf courses, summer camps, and farms. Only in southern Westchester, from White Plains and Rye southward, were there heavy concentrations of people before World War II. West of the Hudson, in Rockland and Orange counties, development was even slower, in part, because of the absence of bridges across the river for a 25-mile stretch between New York City and Peekskill.

Recent developments north of the city have meant expansion of population and industry. Westchester County, the closest to New York, has received the greatest impact. Many of the old estates have been broken up into real estate subdivisions. The extension of the New York State and New England thruways into Westchester and the new limited-access highways in New York City have lured thousands of middle-income commuters to the areas north of the city. They have also lured industries. International Business Machines moved its world headquarters from Madison Avenue to Armonk, above White Plains; later they announced plans to shift nearly 1,000 New York City employees to a new 14-story office building constructed in the White Plains urban-renewal area. Reader's Digest, General Foods, Pepsico, General Motors, Union Carbide, Texaco—these and scores of other concerns have moved north of New York City or have expanded existing facilities in the suburbs. One of the favorite sites is the village of Purchase, an affluent community inland from the Long Island Sound shoreline, where homes range upward from $150,000 and where a number of estates are being turned into office complexes. In Westchester County there is an almost continuous expanse of factories, shopping centers, and stores. To the north, in Putnam County, the old estates and farms have been carved up into sites for homes, offices, and factories, but there are still open spaces available.

The same situation prevails across the Hudson in Rockland and Orange counties where the Tappan Zee Bridge at Tarrytown has brought the area within easy reach of New York City. As settlement and industry continue to expand here, there will be increasing competition for land to meet the demands for highways, parks and reservoirs, and proposed airports and power plants, as well as for the residential, commercial, and industrial growth, which is inevitable since it is only an hour or so driving time from New York City.

In northeastern New Jersey a different situation prevails. The older industrial centers, such as Jersey City, Newark, and Elizabeth, have long been important for chemicals, petroleum refining, steelworks, machinery, and food processing. Newark Bay is the scene of considerable shipbuilding and ship repair. The development of manufacturing has continued since World War II because of excellent transportation facilities and the nearness of markets and other industries that have spilled over onto Staten Island and southward toward Trenton and Philadelphia. The area is laced with railways and superhighways, and to the west of Newark and Paterson are the older "bedroom" towns of New Jersey.

Newark itself was the scene of serious riots in 1967, during which 23 persons were killed and nearly 1,000 injured. The city presents a classic example of urban decay, with nearly 15 percent of the labor force unemployed and 35 percent of the housing classed as substandard. About 10 percent of Newark's population is Puerto Rican, and there are few Spanish-speaking officials within the city government to handle their problems. Unemployment rates in the Puerto Rican community are estimated at greater than 25 percent, while the welfare rate is 30 percent. Another 50 percent of Newark's population is black and, here again, there are problems of underemployment, substandard housing, and other difficulties associated with the older industrial cities of the Northeast.

Population growth has been slow in northeastern New Jersey since World War II. Yet to the southwest there has been considerable expansion; the rail and highway lines between New York and Philadelphia provide superb transport facilities here without the space limitations of the immediate New York City area. A great variety of industrial plants have been located along the Penn Central Railroad and the New Jersey Turnpike from Elizabeth southwestward through New Brunswick to Trenton. This is one of the industrial frontiers of the Northeast. Despite the existence of nonindustrial centers— such as Princeton—and the many farms (producing dairy products, fresh vegetables, poultry, and horticultural specialties for the urban market), what is left of the open spaces is gradually being filled by industries and the inevitable housing developments and shopping centers.

West of New York City, behind the Palisades, are the Hackensack Meadowlands, drained by the Hackensack River, which empties into Newark Bay. This 20,000-acre, poorly-drained area has for years been the dumping ground of garbage and industrial wastes for the surrounding cities. All, or parts, of fourteen New Jersey towns are included within its borders. In 1968, the New Jersey legislature created the Hackensack Meadows Development Commission and charged it with the responsibility of controlling all residential, commercial, recreational, and landfill areas. The Commission responded with a master plan (which excluded downtown Secaucus) calling for specifically planned areas for residential, commercial, and other uses, and preserving or restoring 6,000 acres as open space. One consequence of the plan is the construction, on a 588-acre site, of a sports complex that includes a 76,000 seat stadium, a race track housing 35,000 spectators, and parking for 20,000 cars. Two miles south of the complex, Hartz Mountain Industries is preparing a series of condominium apartments and a new Hilton Inn. Although 50,000 tons of waste continue to be spread each day over the Meadowlands, the region will in time become a built-up part of the urban complex of the New York metropolitan area.

Although manufacturing may, in coming years, continue to decline within New York City itself, there seems little to indicate that industry in the surrounding areas will do the same. On the contrary, both industry and population seem destined to continue their growth northeast into Connecticut, east onto Long Island, north in New York State, and west and southwest in New Jersey. Nor will these peripheral areas be exclusively dependent on New York City. On the one hand, some will develop their own regional centers, and on the other, they will become interconnected, particularly by expressways that bypass the City. The advantages of a mass market, the concentration of research and technical facilities, the well-developed transport media, and the proximity of other industrial establishments that frequently represent suppliers or markets, all combine to perpetuate the New York metropolitan region as one of the industrial centers of the United States.

In early 1975, a comprehensive study was completed by the Regional Plan Commission. The Commission analyzed population change in what it termed the New York Urban Region —an area comprising New York City and twenty-six surrounding counties, including as far south as Ocean County, New Jersey; east through Long Island and along the Connecticut shore to include New Haven; and north through Ulster and Dutchess counties, New York. The Commission found that the population of the Urban Region may have stabilized at about 20 million—some ten years earlier than stabilization had been predicted. There has been, since 1970, a sharp rise in migration into the region of people from Hispanic backgrounds (27,800 a year compared with 14,700 a year average in 1960 to 1970); a decline in the entry of nonwhites (10,800 a year during 1970 to 1974 compared with 66,000 a year average in 1960 to 1970); and a decline of non-Hispanic whites from even the nearer suburbs. By 1990, the Commission predicts, there will be a population drop of nearly one million within New York City itself and the nearer suburbs of such counties as Nassau, Westchester, Hudson, and Union. The net effect of such changes, the study concluded, would be to seriously undermine the economic structure of the New York City area.

By the spring of 1975, New York City was approaching default. Continued deficit budgets had drained the city of its financial reserves, yet the costs of maintaining municipal services continued unabated. Among the major items of expense were education, welfare, police and fire protection, sanitation, and public transportation. Municipal bonds became increasingly difficult to sell; capital construction projects financed by the City slowed down almost to a halt; and the administration began facing crises each time municipal payrolls had to be met. The state government of New York intervened in an effort to assist the City, but it appeared ultimately that only a loan from the federal government could serve to tide New York over until a balanced budget could again be possible.

For a time, federal aid for New York City appeared to have become a major political issue, with the Ford administration admonishing the City for its past extravagances and banks and private investors becoming increasingly alarmed over the prospects of bankruptcy for the nation's largest city. Finally, in November, 1975, a resolution of New York's immediate problems was reached. To underwrite a $6.8 billion financing package for the subsequent two and a half years' borrowing needs, the New York State legislature voted $200 million a year in additional taxes for the City. These included an average 25 percent rise in the income tax of residents, a 50 percent surcharge on the estate tax, and increases in taxes on cigarettes, banks, and various personal services, such as barbershops. This increased funding for the City, amounting to $500 million during the coming two and a half year period, together with various loans—such as those from banks, municipal employee retirement systems, and the State of New York—prompted the federal government to make available $2.3 billion in short-term loans, which the City needed in order to avoid immediate default. But this last-minute resolution of New York City's short-term financial crisis does not solve the long-term issue of balancing the municipal budget in the face of a slow but steady decline in employment, both in the City itself and in the suburbs, and continued heavy operational costs.

THE DELAWARE VALLEY

The city of Trenton, at the head of navigation on the Delaware River, is an old industrial center of 105,000 people. It is located at the boundary between the New York metropolitan and the Delaware Valley urban districts. From Trenton northeast for 60 miles to New York is one expanding industrial area; for 55 miles southwest of Trenton, through Philadelphia and Wilmington, is another, somewhat older region. Across the Delaware from Trenton itself is the newest and second largest of the East Coast steel mills, U.S. Steel's Fairless plant at Morrisville, Pennsylvania.

Philadelphia is situated at the junction of the Delaware and Schuylkill rivers; directly across the Delaware is the satellite city of Camden, New Jersey. Downstream from Philadelphia is a broad waterway in which the channel has been dredged to a minimum depth of 35 feet. For 30 miles southwest of Philadelphia, the Delaware River is lined on its western shore with industries, oil refineries, chemical plants, and cities and towns such as Chester, Wilmington, and New Castle.

The city of Philadelphia received its impetus for growth because of its tidewater location, its proximity to coal deposits, and its development as the eastern terminus of a major transport route through the Appalachian Highlands to the west. Eighty miles northwest of the city, near the headwaters of the

Schuylkill, are extensive anthracite-coal deposits, and the river itself was canalized to bring this coal to Philadelphia. A main line of the Penn-Central Railroad follows the Schuylkill River northwest to Reading, then moves via the Lebanon Valley to Harrisburg on the Susquehanna. From here it continues northwest along the valley of the Juniata River, before climbing the escarpment of the Allegheny Front at Altoona and picking up the headwaters of the Ohio River system. This route, which is much more direct than the Hudson-Mohawk Corridor, has focused considerable trade from the western Pennsylvania and Ohio areas on Philadelphia.

The city is characterized by two phenomena—the great variety of its industries and its relatively limited metropolitan area. Textiles, machinery and machine tools, high-grade paper, food processing, and transportation equipment are among the city's major industries, along with printing and publishing, shoes, and leather. Within the surrounding area are shipbuilding, oil refining, chemicals, and a locomotive plant. Combining the production of shipyards at Philadelphia, Camden, Chester, and Wilmington, the Delaware Valley places first in the nation in shipbuilding. Marcus Hook, located just south of Chester, is a major oil refining center; from Chester to below Wilmington there is an important concentration of chemical plants, many of them associated with the Du Pont Company, whose headquarters are in Delaware.

Outside of Philadelphia, the metropolitan area contains 2.9 million people, nearly 50 percent more than in Philadelphia itself. The area includes the Pennsylvania counties of Delaware, Chester, Montgomery, and Bucks; across the river in New Jersey are Gloucester, Camden, and Burlington counties. Here, as in Long Island, there is a widespread population sprawl, but there are few cities other than Camden, with its 103,000 people. As might be expected, the counties around Philadelphia have increased considerably in population. Chester County, to the south, grew by 32 percent between 1960 and 1970; Burlington County, New Jersey, across the river, by 44 percent; and Bucks County, Pennsylvania, north of Philadelphia, by 35 percent. Bucks County includes not only the

Morrisville steel plant (which itself has attracted subsidiary industries to Bristol and nearby towns) but also considerable open land and old estates that are gradually being transformed into middle-income residential use. Levittown and Fairless Hills are two well-known residential communities, built a short distance from the steel mill but designed also to accommodate other expanding industries to the north of Philadelphia.

The area west of Philadelphia is mostly hilly, with old, well-established towns. Philadelphia does not yet have an arterial belt system; the Pennsylvania Turnpike lies to the north of the city, while the Schuylkill Expressway passes southeast through Philadelphia to link the Pennsylvania Turnpike with the New Jersey Turnpike south of Camden. Because of this alignment, the industrial axis between Trenton and Wilmington is not well served by expressways; although the New Jersey Turnpike parallels this axis, it is some distance to the east, and connections across the Delaware are still inadequate for trucking needs. On the other hand, rail service on the west side of the river, between Trenton and Wilmington, is excellent.

Fifty miles or so north and west of Philadelphia are a ring of smaller cities—Easton, Bethlehem, Allentown, Reading, and Lancaster. The first two, with their resources of iron ore, limestone, and nearby anthracite coal, were early steel-making towns, and even now Bethlehem retains this function. Allentown, Reading, and Lancaster are centers of rich agricultural districts. Although separated from Philadelphia by considerable hill country, these cities are connected to it by rail and highway. Like the ring of cities around Boston, they continue their individual economic existence, although Philadelphia's expanding suburbia is gradually moving toward them.

Across the Delaware River, New Jersey is flat or gently rolling, with no well-established urban centers except Camden. Burlington County, north of Camden, lies athwart the growing industrial New York-Philadelphia axis and has acquired many new manufacturing plants. The large expanses of level land in New Jersey and the presence of the New Jersey Turnpike are generally more of an attraction to industry moving out of downtown Philadelphia than are the areas on the Pennsylvania

side of the river. The Walt Whitman Bridge in South Philadelphia has served to open up Camden and Gloucester counties as residential areas for commuters into the city. For other
sectors of west-central New Jersey, highway connections into
Philadelphia are superior to those from west or north of the
city. Thus, the New Jersey area in recent years has been enjoy-
ing a housing as well as an industrial boom.

Within the Delaware Valley area, industrial growth since
World War II has been steady but not spectacular. The most
outstanding development has been the construction of U.S.
Steel's Morrisville plant, an integrated steel mill employing
6,000 workers, with an annual capacity of about 3.5 million
ingot tons of steel. This half-billion-dollar plant utilizes iron
ore from Cerro Bolivar in Venezuela, coal from Pennsylvania
and West Virginia, and limestone from the Allentown area.
The iron ore is sent by rail in Venezuela from the Cerro Bolivar mines north to the Orinoco River, where it is loaded on
ships for the trip to Pennsylvania. Until the Delaware River
from Philadelphia to Morrisville is sufficiently dredged, most
of the ore boats are being unloaded in Philadelphia, and the
iron ore is taken by rail to the Morrisville plant. In time, both
the Orinoco and the Delaware are to be dredged to sufficient
depths to permit giant ore carriers to ply between Cerro Bolivar and Morrisville. In 1970, U.S. Steel announced plans to
expand the Fairless plant, which included the addition of two
new electric arc furnaces.

The anthracite industry, which once was important to the
industrial development of the Philadelphia area, has declined
considerably, and shipbuilding has been slow since the end of
World War II. On the other hand, the petroleum-refining and
chemical industries have expanded in recent years, although
the growth in production has not been matched by a similar
increase in job opportunities. Locomotives are built at Chester
and railroad cars at Wilmington, while Chrysler has an assembly plant at Newark, Delaware. In the Delaware Valley area,
as around New York, industries have been attracted by the
mass market, the presence of other industries, and the research facilities there; in addition, they have been lured by the

water, rail, and highway network along the 55-mile northeast-southwest axis.

THE BALTIMORE—WASHINGTON CONURBATION

The Delaware Valley industrial area covers most of the state of Delaware but does not extend into Maryland. There is a break of some 40 miles southwest from the Delaware-Maryland line to the Baltimore metropolitan area. Baltimore has a very small immediate industrial area, but it has developed a large trade hinterland and is a major importing and processing center. Washington, on the other hand, has very little industry, except some connected with the city's immediate needs.

The city of Baltimore is located at the head of navigation on the Patapsco River, about 12 miles from Chesapeake Bay and nearly 200 miles from Hampton Roads at the mouth of the Bay. Its location provides an example of a city that has penetrated as far inland as possible while still retaining its seaport functions. It is the center for the rich tidewater agricultural district about Chesapeake Bay (resulting in an early rise in food processing), and was the eastern terminal of the Wilderness Road, over which animals were moved from Ohio to the seacoast up to the time of the Civil War. It is now the headquarters of the Baltimore & Ohio Railroad; like the Penn-Central to the north, it provides access to the Midwest. The B & O follows the Potomac River Valley westward past Harper's Ferry, then cuts across the Alleghenys, traveling into West Virginia to the Ohio River system.

Baltimore has long been a center for processing imported raw materials. Copper smelting, sugar refining, and the production of commercial fertilizer are based on foreign raw materials, as is the city's steel industry. Bethlehem's Sparrows Point plant, built in 1887, is now the largest in the United States, with an annual capacity of 8.2 million ingot tons. The plant utilizes iron ore brought by sea from Bethlehem's mines in Venezuela (not far from those of U.S. Steel), and also from Chile and other Latin American countries. Coal comes from

West Virginia, and limestone from eastern Pennsylvania, with the result that manufacturing costs at Sparrows Point are among the lowest anywhere in the United States. Here, as in the Delaware area, steel production has given rise to various steel-fabricating industries such as shipbuilding, machinery, and machine tools. In 1973, Bethlehem Steel announced plans to expand the Sparrows Point plant by nearly a 3-million-ton capacity.

There is a wide diversity of manufacturing—petroleum refining, canning, textiles, wearing apparel, and printing and publishing. In recent decades, Baltimore has been noted for the production of aircraft and missiles. During World War II, the Martin airplane plant was the city's largest single employer. Bendix, Western Electric, and Westinghouse have large plants in the Baltimore area, and there is a General Motors assembly plant.

The port stands third, behind New York and New Orleans, in value of cargoes handled. It is primarily an importing center, bringing in such foreign products as iron ore, copper, sugar, and nitrate, as well as petroleum and phosphate from the southeastern United States. The city is closer to the Midwest than Philadelphia or New York, and the U.S. Steel Corporation has developed Baltimore as its port for importing foreign ores for its steel plants in the north-central United States. From central New York State and Pennsylvania westward to Nebraska and the Dakotas, freight rates through Baltimore are as low as or lower than those through Philadelphia, New York, or Boston.

The city of Baltimore is ringed on three sides by a magnificent Beltway that has been attracting industry and settlement away from the city proper. In eastern Baltimore the ring is completed by the John F. Kennedy Expressway, which crosses a part of the city, tunnels under the Patapsco River, and continues on to Washington. Downtown Baltimore is also connected with the Beltway to the north by the new Jones Falls Expressway.

Surrounding Baltimore, with its 900,000 people, are approximately 1.2 million more people in Baltimore County, together with Ann Arundell County (where Annapolis is located). Harford County is to the northeast, and Carroll and Howard counties are to the northwest. These surrounding areas are by no means crowded; there are no satellite cities, and although all of the counties except Carroll grew in population between 1960 and 1970 considerably faster than the national average, Baltimore is fortunate in still having considerable space available beyond the Beltway for suburban residential and industrial expansion.

Washington lies 35 miles southeast of Baltimore. Between the two cities, along the Baltimore-Washington Parkway, are located Baltimore's Friendship Airport, College Park (home of the University of Maryland), and a growing agglomeration of bedroom communities. There is, as yet, no continuous string of suburbs between Baltimore and Washington; but they are building toward one another, and the vacant space between them is disappearing quickly. One of these communities is the planned city of Columbia, an 11,600-acre site located about 20 miles northwest of Washington, which by 1970 had a population of over 9,000 and was planned for an eventual population of 110,000.

There is little industry in Washington. Only about 5 percent of the work force is engaged in manufacturing, while one-half are federal government workers. The District initially consisted of a square, ten miles on each side, spanning the Potomac River; but before the Civil War, Virginia reannexed its part of the District south of the River, thereby reducing the District's area by some 40 percent. The Virginia sector is now occupied by the suburbs of Arlington and Alexandria. In 1973, President Nixon signed into law a home rule bill providing for an elected mayor and an elected thirteen-member city council for Washington, but control of the District's budget remains in Congress.

The total population of the District of Columbia dropped by 1 percent between 1960 and 1970; this followed a 5 percent drop in the previous decade. During the twenty-year period of 1950 to 1970, the number of whites in the District dropped by 334,000, while the number of blacks increased by 290,000;

as a result, of Washington's 757,000 people in 1970, 71.1 percent were black. Many of the whites who left the District moved to the suburbs; and here, as in other metropolitan areas of the Northeast, the surrounding counties have grown tremendously. Prince George's and Montgomery counties in Maryland each increased more than 50 percent between 1960 and 1970; in Virginia, Fairfax County grew during the decade from 275,000 to 455,000 (65.5 percent), and Prince William County, from 50,000 to 111,000 (121.5 percent). But Arlington, just across the Potomac from Washington, conformed to the inner-suburb pattern and increased in population less than 7 percent during the 1960s. Two new planned cities have been established—Reston, Virginia, on a 7,200-acre site located near Dulles Airport, about 15 miles west of Washington, and St. Charles, Maryland, 20 miles south of the District in Charles County, Maryland. By 1970, Reston had a population of close to 6,000. As an indication of the rate of growth, the total population of the counties surrounding Washington increased more than 55 percent during the 1960 to 1970 decade.

Washington is located just below the falls of the Potomac; to the northwest and west are the ridges and valleys of the Appalachians, which figured so prominently in Civil War battles; to the east and southeast is the sandy coastal plain of Maryland and Virginia. Washington is an important rail center, the break point between northern and southern railroads. To the north and northwest are the Penn-Central and Baltimore & Ohio lines; to the south run the Southern, and the Richmond, Fredericksburg, and Potomac lines. The latter railroad carries the Seaboard and Atlantic coastline traffic into the city. Washington's National Airport is one of the busiest in the United States, and the Dulles International Airport in Virginia is generally rated as the nation's finest jetport. In addition to government services, Washington is important as a retail trade center, for tourism and conventions, and for education and the arts. It is also important for banking and finance, as a result of the federal government's increasingly complex role in national and international economies.

The Washington metropolitan area faces many of the same

problems as other major cities, problems such as water supply, power, suburbanization, and urban renewal. Due to the lack of industries, however, air pollution is less a concern here than in the other northeastern metropolises. Water comes primarily by aqueduct from upstream on the Potomac, and power depends on coal brought in from the west by rail. Regional planning is handicapped by the existence of three separate political areas—the states of Maryland and Virginia and the District of Columbia. Tax rates, schools, zoning ordinances and other functions vary widely within the Greater Washington area; and while cooperation may not be too difficult in such fields as highway construction or sanitation, it becomes almost out of the question from the standpoint of implementing comprehensive regional-planning programs.

In suburbanization, Washington has the highest per capita number of daily commuters to and from the city of any of the northeastern urban areas. This results from two conditions: first, the fact that the Washington suburbs have few local centers of employment; and second, the high percentage of white-collar workers who daily move in and out of the city. Yet Washington has a very limited rail commutation system and, as yet, has no subway. Most of the commuters must come and go by bus or private car over the limited highway links between the central city and surrounding areas. As noted earlier, a Washington area Metro is under construction, which by 1981 is scheduled to provide a 55-mile subway system for the Greater Washington area, together with a surface-rail network that will be almost equivalent in length.

THE IMAGE OF THE URBAN AXIS

"There are many other large metropolitan areas and even clusters of them in various parts of the United States," Gottmann wrote, "but none of them is yet comparable to Megalopolis in size of population, density of population, or density of activities, be these expressed in terms of transportation, communications, banking operations, or political conferences. Megalopolis provides the whole of America with so many essential services, of the sort a community used to obtain in its 'downtown' section, that it may well deserve the nickname of 'Main Street of the nation.' And for three centuries it has performed this role, though the transcontinental march of settlement has developed along east-west axes perpendicular to this section of the Atlantic seaboard.

"In recent times," he went on to note, "Megalopolis has had concentrated within it more of the Main Street type of functions than ever, and it does not yet seem prepared to relinquish any of them. Witness, for example, the impact of the federal government in Washington, D.C., as it tightens up over many aspects of national life; the continued crowding of financial and managerial functions into Manhattan; New York's dominance of the national markets for mass communication media, which resists all attempts at erosion; and the pre-eminent influence of the universities and cultural centers of Megalopolis on American thinking and policy-making."[4]

As a geographic unit, the Boston-Washington axis faces a number of problems. In the case of many industries that were once paramount here, other parts of the nation can now offer better access to raw materials, power supplies, or markets. Even with the expansion of such fields as electrical machinery and aircraft, this region faces increased industrial underemployment. Tax rates are high, and desirable land for industrial sites is often more expensive here than in other areas of the country. Much of the labor force is highly organized, skilled, and relatively expensive. There is also the problem of low-income, unskilled labor moving into some of the larger cities, which requires additional services and sources of employment.

If industrial employment declines in the Boston-Washington area, job opportunities in the tertiary industries—such as commerce, banking and finance, communications, and government service—continue to grow; but these opportunities tend to be limited to the skilled or educated workers and to be concentrated in the larger urban centers. What becomes of the unskilled or semiskilled workers, the small towns, and

4. Ibid., pp. 7–8.

the older industrial cities? Certainly they are less able to share in the expanding wealth of this part of the nation.

The movement from the cities to the suburbs of the upper- and middle-income groups has raised many difficult questions, in the solution of which two trends have become increasingly apparent. First, there is the increased role of the federal and state governments in community and municipal affairs. Second is the need for regional planning, both within a metropolitan area of one state and, frequently, in an area involving two or more states. But planning *laterally*, across lines of political control, is often extremely difficult. There may be less resistance on the part of political officials in a township or county to limits placed on their authority from groups higher up on the administrative scale than there is to groups at the same administrative level in adjoining areas. Joint meetings may be held and mixed committees established to look into matters of mutual concern—such concerns as sewage control or schools for the mentally retarded—yet when questions of income and expenditure arise, political man, for the most part, turns out to be a highly parochial animal. And yet, as relative distances decline in this part of the Northeast, such parochialism becomes increasingly outdated.

4 The Coastal Lowlands

Between the urban axis and the sea are a series of low, sandy areas, extending from Cape Cod on the north to Cape Charles on the south. In the past, the region's economy was oriented toward general farming, tourism, and commercial fishing. There were many areas of sparse population and poor economic conditions, especially in the central and southern sectors. But the spectacular growth of the urban axis itself in recent decades and of the new highways and bridges in the coastal lowlands has opened much of this area up to new development. Agriculture has become highly specialized; the fishing industry is still of some importance; and the tourist industry has expanded tremendously. In addition, manufacturing has developed, particularly in eastern Long Island, and parts of the coastal lowlands are being used for year-round residents.

The lowlands are considered in this chapter in four sectors: Cape Cod and the islands; Long Island east of New York City; southeastern New Jersey beyond the New York-Philadelphia axis; and the Delmarva Peninsula from south of Wilmington to Cape Charles, Virginia. Prior to these regional analyses, however, consideration will be given to the three predominant activities.

AGRICULTURAL SPECIALIZATION FOR THE URBAN MARKET

Agricultural production in the coastal lowlands is geared to perishable products designed for direct human consumption. The great attraction of this area is its proximity to the mass urban market, a market in which many people have above-average incomes. The farms are specialized and efficient, most of them engaging in one of four activities—horticulture, poultry husbandry, dairying, and the raising of market garden crops.

The soils are not naturally of high fertility, but they respond well to fertilization. Although yearly precipitation is generally high, the sandy soils tend to be droughty, and irrigation is often necessary during short periods in the summer. The region has in recent years suffered repeatedly from tropical hurricanes, as well as from high winds associated with coastal storms. There is practically nothing in this area that could not be grown as well or better in other parts of the United States, but the nearby market provides the added incentive.

The rising economic level of people in both the urban axis and the coastal lowlands has contributed to the growth of the horticulture industry. Trees, shrubs, plants, cut flowers, Christmas trees—these and similar items bring high returns per acre, but they also require considerable investment and skill. Here, proximity to the consumer market and to a labor supply is of great importance. Not only are returns high but the farms—which are close to urban areas—may in time be sold at a high prices for conversion of the land into residential use.

Another specialized industry is poultry husbandry. The poultry are fed entirely on imported feeds, thereby reducing the acreage needed for farms. Because of the generally low margin of profit, many of the small-time poultry producers have been forced out of business. At the same time, the larger ones face competition in the market of eggs and of frozen broilers from poultrymen in other parts of the country, who produce for less and send their products to the Northeast.

Dairying is important, particularly on the upper Delmarva Peninsula and in Burlington County, New Jersey, east of Philadelphia. As in the case of poultry husbandry, more and more dairy farmers are coming to depend on imported feed. Some farms also have gone into the production of beef cattle, but conditions in the coastal lowlands are hardly competitive with those in other parts of the country.

One of the interesting aspects of dairying is the existence of milkshed areas for the major cities. These areas are established by municipal or state legislation for public health purposes. Within each area, fluid milk and, frequently, fresh cream may be produced and sold to the urban area subject to inspection and licensing by responsible authorities. Farmers within the milkshed must comply with certain rules and regulations, but those beyond its boundaries may not be licensed to sell fresh milk or cream to the city. A great deal of political jockeying goes on in the delimitation of milkshed boundaries; some areas lie within the milkshed of two or three cities. The northern sector of the Delmarva Peninsula, west of Wilmington, serves both Philadelphia and Baltimore; south of this is a New York-Philadelphia-Baltimore milkshed; while still farther south, in the Cambridge-Salisbury region, is a Philadelphia-Baltimore-Washington milkshed.

Market garden crops—that is, fresh fruits and vegetables —are also important. Southeastern Massachusetts leads the nation in the production of cranberries; while tomatoes, asparagus, strawberries, lettuce, and other fruits and vegetables are grown in New Jersey (the Garden State) and on the Delmarva Peninsula. Crops such as these have high labor requirements; and in addition to local summer help, migrant workers are brought in, particularly at harvest time. Much of the produce is sold fresh to the urban markets, but canning and freezing are also an important aspect of production. Located in southern New Jersey is Seabrook Farms, the country's largest grower and packager of frozen vegetables. Not only does this organization harvest over 20,000 acres of its own produce each year but it also contracts to buy up the output of many neighboring farms.

THE FISHING INDUSTRY

The fishing industry along the coastal lowlands has failed to keep pace with other economic developments in the area. The ocean fleet has suffered from outmoded equipment, lack of capital investment, pollution, state laws that support inefficiencies, foreign imports, and the competition of foreign fleets in the waters beyond the 12-mile exclusive fishing limit. Lacking the government supports that agriculture enjoys, the Northeast's fishing industry can supply only a portion of the market's demands, and many of the fish products are imported from Canada, Japan, or Western Europe.

Gloucester, New Bedford, Point Judith (Rhode Island), and Boston are the major ports for ocean fishing in New England; followed by Portland, Newport, Provincetown, and Stonington, Connecticut. Flounder, cod, ocean perch, whiting, and mackerel are the principal food fishes harvested, but the stocks of all of these species have been declining in recent years due to the heavy fishing by foreign fleets. Haddock, once a very valuable species, has all but disappeared. Yet, through international agreements, quotas are now placed on the quantity of certain species that can be fished for by aliens off the Northeast. United States fishermen claim that: 1) the quotas are still too high to permit the stocks to recover from the overfishing of the past; 2) inspection and enforcement procedures are inadequate; and 3) foreign fleets tend to exceed their allotted quotas. In addition to the high-priced food fish, there are the "trash fish," particularly menhaden, which are processed for fish meal and used as an additive for poultry and cattle feed and for fish oil. These species do not appear to be in danger of depletion. Some New England vessels travel north to fish off the coasts of Canada, but the majority stay close to their home ports. Yet their harvesting ability, even in coastal waters, tends to be overshadowed by the very large ships of the foreign, distant-water fleets.

Shellfishing is also an important activity, with scallops, clams, quahaugs, and lobsters representing the principal species. Both pollution and heavy fishing have affected the catches in inshore waters, and in recent years increased attention has been given to deep-water lobsters and to ocean quahaugs. Some experiments have been made with shellfish farming: the shellfish are either grown on rafts or strings, or portions of the bottom are reserved for production. Although the unit price of shellfish is high, there has been little success in commercial ventures. The fisheries are still looked upon by the public as a common property resource, and legislatures are loathe to close off saltwater areas to public use. Another form of accommodation in congested waters is depuration, a process whereby shellfish are cleansed of their pollutants by natural or artificial means. There are few depuration efforts now being carried out on a commercial scale.

The New England catch, which amounted to over 1 billion pounds in the mid-1950s, dropped to less than 400 million pounds by 1974. New Bedford, second in catch landed for ports in the nation a decade ago, dropped to seventh place by 1974. Some bright spots, however, were in Rhode Island landings, particularly those at Point Judith, where perhaps the most successful fishermen's cooperative in the United States is located. Between 1964 and 1974, the volume of catch increased nearly 200 percent, and the value of the catch increased three and a half times. This growth results from short trips, flexible fishing (the skippers can quickly switch from one species to another in response to changing market prices), and sound management of the cooperative.

South of New England, fishing ports are smaller in terms of both volume and value of catch. Among these are Montauk, Long Island; Fort Monmouth, Atlantic City; Cape May, New Jersey; Lewes, Delaware; and Ocean City, Maryland. Menhaden is the most important species landed. Oysters rank first in value among the shellfish. The bulk of these are Chesapeake Bay oysters, but some are also taken from Long Island Sound, Delaware Bay, and lower New York Bay. Long Island Sound oysters have been declining in quantity since 1950.

The impact of fishing on the overall economy of the coastal lowlands is not great. The Northeastern states in 1974 had a combined total of 21,000 full-time fishermen, and 33,000 part-time ones. Local impact is strong along parts of the Maine coast, where lobstering is an important activity; in the oystering towns of Chesapeake Bay; in the clam and oyster townships of eastern Long Island; and in individual port communities such as Gloucester, Point Judith, and Lewes. In some states, as noted earlier, legislation exists that is designed to enforce inefficient methods of fishing, thereby increasing employment opportunities. An example of this is the Maryland law prohibiting oystering by motorized vessels. The sailing boats of the Solomon Islands oyster fleet are picturesque but hardly in keeping with the image of a modern, technologically efficient industry. On the other hand, sports fishing is an ever-growing industry, with party boats, charter boats, and other activities often competing with the commercial fishermen both for ocean space and for the catch.

A hopeful sign for the Northeast's fishing industry is the imminence of a 200-mile exclusive fisheries zone around the United States. Such a move may come either through international agreement, at the Third Law of the Sea Conference, or through unilateral action on the part of the United States. Once such a zone has been constituted, fishing by aliens off the United States coasts can be regulated. Conservation measures can be instituted by the United States and enforced by United States vessels to the maximum offshore limit of the fishing grounds. As the capacity of the United States fishing fleet expands, certain preferred species such as flounder, scallops, and (assuming they recover) haddock can be designated as completely off limits to foreign fishing. While exclusive or preferential rights to the offshore resources will not solve all the economic problems of the Northeast's fisheries, the imposition of the 200-mile limit should greatly help protect the resource and pave the way for a more viable fishing industry to develop.

THE IMPACT OF TOURISM

The existence of long, sandy beaches, protected inlets and islands, historic seacoast towns, and special tourist meccas so close to the Boston-Washington axis has meant the creation and maintenance of a rich summer-tourist industry in the coastal lowlands, an industry that is constantly seeking to extend its seasons both earlier into the spring and later into the fall. Some places, such as Atlantic City, maintain a semblance of business as usual right through the winter, although the overall tourist trade in Atlantic City has declined considerably in recent years.

The Northeast coast has long been a summer vacation area. Bar Harbor, Cape Cod, Narragansett Pier, the Hamptons, and the Jersey shore have for nearly a century attracted summer vacationists. The Old Colony and New England Steamship lines, the massive hotels with their stately dining rooms, the ocean piers and the yacht clubs, the clusters of summer cottages, all attest to the traditional importance of this region as a tourist area. The increased affluence of the Northeast and the shorter working hours have meant still greater numbers of recreationists than in the past, but to some extent their objectives have changed. This change affects both the distribution and extent of income derived from tourism and the relative advantages the Northeast now enjoys with respect to other summer vacation areas.

The recreation industry may be divided in several ways. As noted earlier, one division is between public and private recreation. Private recreation involves individually owned homes, cottages, and camps to which families and individuals return year after year. This has been a long-term pattern for many seaside areas; children and grandchildren grow up and return each year with their families to the same locale.

Public recreation is much more complex. There is, on the one hand, somewhat of a mixed public-private situation in which families rent cottages, camps, or hotel accommodations on a fairly regular basis each year. Or, an individual or a family may lease a summer resort facility in advance for a season or for several weeks but not return a second year. Further along the spectrum are the short-term tourists who leave on a trip, planning to spend a night or several days at whatever accommodations are available; these may include motels, guest houses, or campsites. For these, reservations may or may not have been made in advance. Finally, there are the day-trip vacationers who head for the beaches, marinas, picnic sites, and other attractions to spend only a few hours before returning home.

For each of these categories there are different demands for facilities and different means by which income is earned by the recreation community. The private recreation areas tend to be economically more stable, with a fairly level demand for carpenters, food stores, marinas, beach clubs, and so on. This is also true for the public-private category, although more facilities are expected here in the form of restaurants, shops, and summer theaters than in the predominantly private areas.

The short-term vacationists are perhaps the most demanding in facilities expected, but they also tend to be relatively heavy spenders. If they go away on a short trip (and do not plan to spend the whole time driving), they are often prepared to meet local prices in order to enjoy the sailboats, restaurants, beach facilities, and other activities the vacation spot has to offer on short notice. They tend to go where such facilities are readily available, and the result is often severe weekend and holiday congestion at certain favored areas.

Such tourists present special problems to the vacation spots. For example, facilities must be expanded to handle the expected influx; yet the magnitude of the influx may well depend on the weather. A rainy Saturday or Sunday in New York may seriously affect the size of the crowds out on Long Island or at the Jersey shore resorts; rain at the resorts themselves, but not in New York, may also affect the size but generally not as much. A forecast of rain for the weekend is also serious. Many resort owners have taken out rain insurance to protect themselves, but in writing the policy for a certain weekend or holiday the owner must weigh the risks against which he is seeking protection. Rain in New York, rain at the resort, a forecast of rain, and the problem of how much rain—the more exigencies he includes, the higher the premium.

Not all these summer tourists contribute much to the local

economy. There are those who purchase supplies before leaving home, drive to a resort area, and spend their nights in a tent or a trailer. Because of the rising costs in accommodations, food, and other goods at summer vacation spots, the number of such nonpaying vacationists is on the rise. Local communities take steps against an influx of such groups by requiring parking permits at town beaches, prohibiting overnight parking or sleeping on public beaches, and patrolling town roads watching for illegal campsites.

Finally, there are the tourists who stay away from home only a few hours at a time. On pleasant, summer weekend days the cities of the coastal lowlands explode with automobiles, buses, and trains heading for the seashore, the lakes, and other attractions. Again, these recreation facilities are in great demand, and considerable wealth changes hands on Saturdays and Sundays between Memorial and Labor days at such public resorts as Jones Beach, Nantasket, Asbury Park, and Ocean City, Maryland.

Competition for the business of the summer vacationist is very keen, not only among parts of the coastal lowlands themselves, but also between the Northeast and other areas. More and more, the tourist tends to be lured away from traditional haunts by other prospects, such as the American West, the Canadian Maritime provinces, the Caribbean, or Europe. The energy crisis and the rising cost of gasoline may affect the habit of driving long distances to a seashore or lakeside resort in the Northeast. This trend may be accentuated by the availability of package tours to other parts of the world.

Although forecasters have, for at least the past decade and a half, warned against the overdevelopment of tourist facilities in such areas as Cape Cod, the Jersey shore, and eastern Maryland, the summer recreation business still seems to be in a healthy state. New bridges, tunnels, and limited-access highways have been built that make practically all areas of the coastal lowlands accessible to the summer vacationist. Vacations, whether for the length of a season, a month, or a day, are still very much a part of the American way of life.

REGIONAL DIFFERENCES

Cape Cod and the Islands

East and southeast of the Boston-Brockton-New Bedford urban axis lie Cape Cod, Martha's Vineyard, and Nantucket. The Cape's various attractions make it an almost ideal tourist area. It has long stretches of sandy beach, over 200 fresh-water ponds, protected waters for boating, and a summer climate several degrees cooler than that on the mainland to the west. It also capitalizes on the quaint charm of its villages, the seafaring atmosphere, and the lighthouses, colonial churches, and fishing piers that dot the landscape. Over one million tourists visit the Cape each year.

The tourist industry has had its inevitable effects. The highway from Hyannis to Chatham is jammed with motels, restaurants, antique stores, drive-ins, and similar attractions. Provincetown, Falmouth, and other towns are virtually remade in the summer months for the tourist trade. Yet there are large areas of Cape Cod, away from the beaches, that have been relatively untouched. A broad expanse of pine barrens north of Falmouth has remained a military reservation since World War II. On the outer Cape is the 27,000-acre Cape Cod National Seashore, designed to preserve the natural beauty of the outer beach between Chatham and Truro.

On the Cape there is some agriculture (cranberries, vegetables, blueberries, poultry husbandry), local manufacturing, and fishing (in Provincetown). Between 1960 and 1970, Cape Cod's year-round population increased by 40 percent; for the twenty-year period 1950 to 1970, it more than doubled. Some of its people are engaged in the tourist business; others have come there to retire; but quite a number are commuters, particularly to the Greater Boston area. The pleasant year-round living is now less than two hours by car from Boston.

Martha's Vineyard has 6,000 people, and Nantucket 3,800. Here, even more than on Cape Cod, the economies are dependent on tourism and the incomes of retired persons. In contrast to Cape Cod, these islands have not seen substantial increases in their populations, in part because of their limited accessibility (ferry service or air) and the limited availability of land for sale. The relative remoteness of the two islands is, of course, a major component of their charm.

Forty miles to the west of Martha's Vineyard is Block Island, Rhode Island, another summertime retreat with a year-round population of about 500. Ferries connect the island area with the Rhode Island mainland and, in summer, with Connecticut and Long Island also. There are few attractions here except sand, sea, and serenity.

Long Island

Western Long Island has, to some extent, already been covered (see page 67). Nassau County, which lies in the center of Long Island, is industrially an extension of the New York area. Along its shoreline, in Manhasset, Glen Cove, and Oyster Bay on the north, with their millionaires' estates, the land has long been occupied by summer and year-round users. The Rockaways, Long Beach, and Jones Beach on the south cater to the less affluent. Many of the north shore estates have been turned over to institutions and developed as public parks or broken up into building developments. In southern Nassau County—as along the Westchester and southwest Connecticut shores—there is considerable friction between the seasonal vacationist, who has a cottage or camp for an extended period, and the crowds of day visitors who flock to the shores.

Nassau County is primarily a bedroom area for 1.4 million people. One of its most noted developments is Levittown, ten miles east of the city limits of Queens, which contains over 17,000 single-family homes. Housing and shopping developments have devoured most of the remaining open land in the county.

Suffolk County occupies the eastern two-thirds of Long Island. Its sandy soils are better suited for agriculture, and here one finds considerable market gardening—potatoes, cauliflower, cabbages, sweet corn, tomatoes—as well as poultry husbandry. The value of its agricultural produce in 1969 was $50 million. Industry, attracted by the vacant land and proximity to research centers in the New York City area, has also expanded here, particularly aircraft, space, and defense systems. Suffolk County has considerable scope for development, with three times the area of Nassau County and 80 percent of the population. Its hundreds of miles of beaches are well adapted to the summer tourist industry. Names such as Fire Island, the Hamptons, and Montauk Point are well known to vacationers, as are Gardiners, Plum, and Fishers islands. Montauk Point, at the easternmost tip of Long Island, lies 125 miles from Manhattan and 33 miles beyond a connecting expressway to New York City. Eastern Long Island is by no means as intensively developed for tourism as Cape Cod, even though it lies closer to the New York metropolitan area. For one thing, it lacks Cape Cod's historic charm; for another, it must compete with the vacation spots closer to the city. With the eventual completion of the Long Island Expressway to Riverhead, more and more New Yorkers will discover eastern Long Island as a summer vacation spot, and more and more tourist facilities will be developed there.

Southeastern New Jersey

The region east and south of the New York-Delaware River axis is a level or gently rolling sandy area, with few lakes or rivers. In its western part it is particularly level, with a greater admixture of clay in the soil. East and southeast of Camden this inner belt has been developed as an important market garden center.

The nine counties that make up southeastern New Jersey include about 2 million people. With the exception of Camden, the only important urban area is Atlantic City—a major tourist center with 60,000 people. Located sixty miles southeast of Philadelphia on an offshore bar, Atlantic City, with its hotels, boardwalks, and amusement centers, is the largest city in the Northeast devoted almost exclusively to serving the tourist trade. About 15 million persons each year visit the city;

a figure that, as noted earlier, is well below that of several decades ago. It is connected by rail and highway with Philadelphia and, via the Garden State Parkway, with New York, 115 miles away.

Almost the entire Jersey coast is lined with sand dunes and offshore bars. The Garden State Parkway, a limited-access highway, parallels the coast from Staten Island all the way to Cape May, which is the southernmost point of New Jersey. In the north are many noted resorts, such as Atlantic Highlands, Long Branch, and Asbury Park, as well as scores of others. In years to come, New Jersey, like eastern Long Island, stands to benefit from the expanding summer vacation industry.

Ocean County, New Jersey, which nearly doubled in population between 1960 and 1970, is experiencing a new phenomenon; namely, limits on population expansion brought about by decisions on the part of federal and state agencies. The county, some 60 miles south of New York, has accounted in recent years for about one-sixth of all new housing built in New Jersey. Much of the vacant land is owned by major developers.

In 1974, the Ocean County Sewerage Authority requested the Federal Environmental Protection Agency to authorize sewage facilities for nearly 250,000 new people in the central part of the county by 1990. But the agency, feeling that such an expansion would jeopardize national air quality standards, authorized facilities for less than half the expected growth, with a 1984 cutoff date for expansion. Thus, Ocean County may eventually be forced to stop new construction. A somewhat analogous situation exists in the town of East Hampton, Long Island, where local officials have moved to curtail future growth by increasing its minimum lot size from one to two acres. In this case, Suffolk County officials are concerned with the limited underground water supply and the possibility of endangering the area's tourist economy by extensive subdivisions. Such restrictions to growth may become an increasing phenomenon in the coastal lowlands as pressures grow for preserving environmental conditions as they are. A recent court decision that these restrictions to growth are illegal if designed to keep out lower-income families could result in civil rights litigation and one or more test cases of these new regulations.

The total value of agricultural produce from the nine counties of southeastern New Jersey came to $130 million in 1969, of which over $42 million was from poultry and poultry products. There is ample space here for expansion of agricultural specialization. Even in the 3,000-square-mile pine barrens there are many clearings for truck gardens or cranberry bogs. The important elements for production are fertilizers and transport facilities rather than variations in the land itself.

North of the pine barrens are the Fort Dix military reservation and McGuire Air Force Base, a military air transport service installation. Industry in southeastern New Jersey is concentrated in three areas: immediately south of New York, where there has been expansion eastward from the New Brunswick-Perth Amboy district; across the Delaware River from Philadelphia; and south of Wilmington, along the eastern shore of Delaware Bay.

The Delmarva Peninsula

This region—comprising the three counties of Delaware, nine in eastern Maryland, and two in Virginia—has a total population of 850,000 and agricultural produce valued in 1969 at over $340 million, of which $230 million was from poultry and poultry products. The topography is much like that of southeastern New Jersey but with a better developed drainage system of rivers and creeks. Only below the mouth of Delaware Bay does one encounter the long line of offshore bars typical of the Atlantic coast of New Jersey. The Chesapeake Bay shoreline has many inlets and islands but few sandy beaches.

The state of Delaware is an expanding agricultural and industrial area. In the north, New Castle County, containing Wilmington and Newark, is a part of the Philadelphia urbanized area. Kent County, in central Delaware, and Sussex, in the south, are more typical of the coastal lowlands. The scope of agricultural development here may be seen by the $130 million worth of agricultural products produced in these counties in 1969. Sussex County is the leading poultry producer of the counties in the northeastern United States.

This rich agricultural area extends across the state line to include five counties in eastern Maryland—Caroline, Dorchester, Wicomico, Somerset, and Worcester. This is an area of few large towns and modest population growth, relatively isolated and without superhighways or great industrial development. Market garden crops move overnight to the urban centers of the north or to the canneries of Baltimore. The longer growing season permits this area to send fresh vegetables to the northern cities earlier than New Jersey or New York. Dairying is important in the northern counties of Maryland, but poultry is of far greater value.

The two Virginia counties of the Peninsula have, between them, just over 40,000 people. Potatoes are important here, but there is little dairying, poultry husbandry, or industry. These counties were extremely isolated until the opening of the Chesapeake Bay Bridge-Tunnel, and even now their potential does not appear great. The land is flat and the soil relatively infertile, and industry, should it come to the Peninsula, would more likely be located farther north, closer to markets and labor supply.

The tourist business is not as well developed on the Delmarva Peninsula as in the more northern parts of the coastal lowlands because of the historical evolution of the industry and because of isolation from major population centers. Rehoboth Beach, Delaware, and Ocean City, Maryland, have long been known as vacation spots, but there are relatively few other towns that have attracted large numbers of urban dwellers. Summers tend to be hot at this latitude, and the tourist from Wilmington, Baltimore, and Washington will, if he has the chance, probably seek out cooler areas. The opening of the Bay Bridge, however, is bringing more and more weekend visitors to the Delaware and Maryland ocean resorts from Baltimore and Washington, while the Chesapeake Bay Bridge-Tunnel has a similar effect for the Norfolk area. Many residents about Chesapeake Bay are also attracted to the inlets and islands along the northern part of the eastern shore, where conditions for pleasure boating are almost ideal and where there are many camps, cottages, and amusement parks.

No cities, only regional towns, are on the Delmarva Peninsula south of Wilmington. Among these are Dover and Milford, Delaware, and Cambridge and Salisbury, Maryland. Here, for the first time, one encounters a sizeable proportion of blacks in a nonurban population, ranging from 15 percent of the total population in Kent County, Delaware to 53 percent in Northampton County, Virginia.

The northern part of the Peninsula should witness continued economic growth in coming years because of industrial development along Delaware River and Delaware Bay and the expansion of industry between Wilmington and Baltimore. Industry and agriculture should continue strong in the central area, centering on Sussex and the adjacent Maryland counties. The slowest growth would seem to be along the eastern shore of Chesapeake Bay, particularly the southern part, where at present there is little to attract manufacturing, agricultural expansion, tourism, or even residential development.

One other sector of the coastal lowlands consists of the so-called Manor Counties of Maryland, particularly Charles, Calvert, and St. Mary's counties, which lie southeast of Washington, D.C. These counties are on peninsulas formed by the Chesapeake Bay on the east and the Patuxent and Potomac rivers on the south and west. For many years they have been sleepy agricultural areas, specializing in tobacco and with no cities and little population growth. From Solomons Island, St. Mary's City, and other coastal towns, oyster fishermen ply their trade; and in the northern part of Calvert County are Chesapeake Beach and other resorts for Washington and Baltimore. But up until recently, the 120,000 people of the Manor Counties have been largely undisturbed by technology and change.

The expansion of Washington—and, to some extent, of Baltimore as well—is beginning to affect the area. Between 1960 and 1970, populations in the three counties grew by about one-third. Charles County is less than 30 miles from Washington; and the long coastline along creeks, rivers, and the bay, the well-developed road network, and the availability of open land here are coming to serve as a magnet for Washington exurbanites who desire a weekend retreat, a summer cottage, or even a place from which they can commute to the city. Even Baltimore is only 50 miles away, and the beaches along Chesapeake Bay are far closer to Washington and Baltimore than are Rehoboth Beach and Ocean City along the Atlantic coast. The Patuxent Naval Air Station, at the mouth of the Patuxent River, is a large installation, with many base personnel in surrounding towns. Thus the Manor Counties appear destined to become suburbanized, as have Bucks County, Pennsylvania; Suffolk County, Long Island; and Orange County, northwest of New York City.

5 The Interior Highlands

West and north of the urban axis are the interior highlands, stretching from northern Maine to southwestern Pennsylvania and Maryland, a distance of nearly 900 miles. The general trend of these uplands is northeast-southwest. The region is traversed by a number of rivers flowing down to the sea, such as the Penobscot, the Merrimack, the Delaware, and the Susquehanna. The valleys of these rivers form important transportation lines, and in these valleys are located many of the important cities of the highlands, including Manchester (New Hampshire), Albany, Utica, Binghamton, Harrisburg, and Pittsburgh. Within the region is also a broad lowland area, the Ontario Plain of western New York, where Rochester and Buffalo are located.

Many of the natural resources of the interior highlands are no longer utilized to the extent that they once were, leading some regions to economic decline and population loss. Among these resources are anthracite and bituminous coal, marble and granite, water power, timber, and agricultural land. On the other hand, the highlands have profited from their proximity to the urban axis and, in western Pennsylvania, to the Ohio iron and steel areas. The highlands are being progressively opened up to new interstate highways, so that economic developments are now pointing toward tourism, dairying, and light manufactures. Nor have the older pursuits entirely disappeared, for the paper industry is still strong in Maine, as are the textile and shoe industries in western New York State and the bituminous coal industry in Pennsylvania. Here, as in other parts of the Northeast, tradition and change are closely intermingled.

In the regional discussion of the interior highlands, the area will be subdivided into three parts: the northern uplands, comprising northern New England and the Adirondacks; the Mohawk-Ontario Plain Lowlands; and the Appalachian Highlands.

THE NORTHERN UPLANDS

Stretching across northern New England and New York State is a rugged area of hills and low mountains. On the east they border the Atlantic along an extremely rugged coastline, and in the west they dip down to the St. Lawrence Lowland. Winters tend to be relatively severe—most of the northern area has a growing season of less than four months—and soils in general are poor. There are many rivers and lakes providing water for power, industry, or recreation. Most of the virgin timber is gone, and reforestation efforts have been spotty. Quarrying has declined greatly in value in recent decades, as have many branches of industry. Tourism, on the other hand, continues to expand.

Along the southern sector of the coastal region there is a string of cities and towns from northeastern Massachusetts through New Hampshire and southern Maine. Portsmouth, New Hampshire, has long benefited from the existence of a naval shipyard employing over 7,000 people, as well as Pease Air Force Base. Although the shipyard still exists, the Air Force base has been phased out, with a movement of some 2,000 base personnel away from the Portsmouth area. Portland, Maine (45 miles northeast of Portsmouth) is a trade and manufacturing center as well as a seaport and fishing town. The principal product handled by the port is petroleum, either for use in Maine or for transport by pipeline from Portland to Montreal.

The economic potential in Maine's coastal region is based largely on fishing, tourism, and power. Fishing is carried out principally from three ports: Portland; Rockland, on Penobscot Bay; and Eastport, close to the Canadian border. In 1973, the state had a fishery catch valued at $43 million, over half of which came from lobsters. Although the total value of commercial fisheries in Maine is considerably less than that of Massachusetts, the industry is of greater relative importance here than in the Bay State, and Maine lobsters are packed in ice and sent to all parts of the United States.

From Bar Harbor south there are a number of summer resorts to which tourists are attracted by the cool weather, the scenic shoreline, and the various summer features, such as theaters, art galleries, and fishing wharves. At the northernmost point on the coast is Passamaquoddy Bay, where plans still exist, at least on paper, for a joint United States-Canadian project that will harness the tides to provide 1 million kilowatts of power a day for the northeastern United States and adjacent Canada.

Within 75 miles of the seacoast are other urban centers of the New England Uplands. The Merrimack Valley contains the industrial cities of Concord, Manchester, and Nashua, New Hampshire and Lowell, Lawrence, and Haverhill, Massachusetts. Historically, this was an area of textiles and shoe manufactures. Prior to World War I, the factories of the Valley employed nearly 150,000 people. But here, as elsewhere in New England, the years since 1919 have witnessed industrial change and decline. By 1939, manufacturing employment was down to 71,000. The enormous Amoskeag cotton mills in Manchester, which at their peak employed over 17,000 people, were closed down in 1935, never to reopen. Only with World War II was the Merrimack Valley able to recapture some of its former industrial strength. Since that war, such industries as electrical products and machinery have expanded in the area, but the total number employed in manufacturing is still one-third below the level of fifty-five years ago. The closing of giant textile mills in Lawrence and Nashua has accentuated the changing economic position of this industrial area. These older manufacturing centers are still dotted with mill and factory buildings, many of them partially occupied by stores and small manufacturing outfits, and with rows of what were homes of millworkers. They are plagued by fantastic tax problems brought on by the loss of industry and the growing need for municipal services.

Northeast of the Merrimack Valley are smaller urban centers in Maine, which were also dependent on textile and shoe manufacturers and have also suffered industrial change and decline in the past several decades. These cities include Auburn, Lewiston, Augusta, Waterville, and Bangor. All of them are on rivers draining the wooded areas of central Maine, and all are in a position to utilize water power and to process the logs brought downstream from the interior. Over 85 percent of Maine is covered with forests; but much of the available timber is gone, and small-scale waterpower sites have, in general, been found to be no longer economically feasible, so that these centers too must look for new industries. There are paper and pulp mills and some electrical products manufactures. Bangor for years was fortunate in being the site of the massive Dow Air Force Base, with its nearly 13,000 personnel. In 1968, however, the Air Force closed down operations, and the base is now used as a municipal field by the city of Bangor. It has been hoped that the airport might in time be developed as an alternative to New York City as a terminus for some transatlantic flights, thereby relieving part of New York's congestion. Connecting flights could take the overseas passengers to other points in North America. To date, however, such plans have not been implemented.

Moving farther inland, there are few important population centers remaining in New England. The interior of Maine is rugged and covered largely with cut-over forest. There are many lakes, such as Moosehead, Belgrade Lakes, and Sebago. In northwestern Maine the Allagash River, flowing northward to the St. Lawrence, has often been mentioned as the site of a major hydroelectric power and recreation complex. In addition to tourism and lumbering, the principal source of income is pulp and paper manufacturing. The St. Regis Paper Company, in its various plants throughout Maine, employs over

20,000 people. Oxford Paper has a large plant at Rumford; Great Northern Paper, at Millinocket; and International Paper, at Livermore Falls. Paper and pulp are also important in the Bangor area and along the St. Croix River in northeastern-most Maine. Container and packaging manufacture is the nation's third largest industry (topped only by automobiles and steel), and as it continues to grow, northern and central Maine will be able to realize increasing economic benefits.

In northeastern Maine is the Aroostook Valley, an island of fertile, sandy soils admirably suited to the growing of potatoes. The area is linked with Portland by the Bangor and Aroostook Railroad and is an important center for the production and export of seed potatoes to other parts of the United States. Here, also, are two major Air Force bases, Presque Island and Loring. This isolated region, 150 miles north of Bangor, has been linked with southern Maine through the completion of Interstate Highway 95 from Bangor to the New Brunswick border.

Most of the state of Maine is a peninsula extending north-ward into Canada. The economic potential of northern and central Maine has many facets in common with that of eastern Canada, as evidenced by such activities as lumbering, power development, tourism, and manufacturing—particularly in the pulp and paper fields. Joint investments in such enterprises as transportation and power development would seem a wise policy to follow in the further utilization of this frontier area.

New Hampshire, north of the Merrimack industrial area, is also sparsely settled. But it enjoys the twin advantages of the White Mountains and fairly close proximity to the southern New England urban centers. This is a recreational area *par excellence,* with year-round activities centering on such spots as Bretton Woods, North Conway, and Lake Winnipesaukee. Over in Vermont, the Green Mountains, which extend north-south through the state, are also important tourist attractions, although less spectacular than the Presidential Range of the White Mountains. Vermont has small manufacturing towns such as Springfield, White River Junction, and St. Johnsbury. Granite from Barre and marble from the Rutland area were once important segments of Vermont's economy, but today these rocks find little use in construction or facing. Crushed granite for roadstone and concrete aggregate is an important business, and some asbestos and talc also are mined.

Vermont's core area is the Champlain Lowland in the northwestern part of the state between Burlington and Rutland. Here, in a limestone valley, is the center of the state's dairy industry, as well as its two largest cities—Burlington, on Lake Champlain, and Rutland, 60 miles to the south. In spite of its cold winters, the Champlain Lowland provides a favorable environment for dairy cattle. Vermont lies within the milksheds of both New York and Boston. Because of its proximity to these urban markets, its fluid milk can compete with supplies coming in from western New York or the Wisconsin dairy area.

Agriculture other than dairying brings little income to Vermont. Industry is of limited extent also, and the state's principal source of revenue is tourism, which is carried on throughout the year. Vermont's population, which increased only 3 percent in the 1950 to 1960 decade, grew by over 14 percent between 1960 and 1970. The increase is due, in part, to the state's expanding recreation industry, particularly winter sports, but also to the fact that it has become a favorite retirement place. Many of the homes and farms have been bought up by out-of-staters and are inhabited year-round.

One feature of the three northern New England states has been the gradual decline in passenger train service over the past few decades. One by one, the railroads serving this area— the Rutland, the Central Vermont, the Maine Central, the Bangor & Aroostook, and the Boston & Maine—have abandoned passenger service. In Vermont and northern New Hampshire the only passenger service is supplied by two trains a day in each direction between Montreal and New York City via Burlington, northeastern Vermont, and the Connecticut River Valley. In northern Maine, one passenger train a day in each direction crosses the state on the Canadian Pacific Railway between Montreal and St. John, New Brunswick.

The uplands of Vermont continue south into western Massachusetts and Connecticut as the Berkshires and the Taconics. Here again tourism is an economic mainstay. Some of the charming towns—such as Lee, Salisbury, and Sharon—contain many homes of the well-to-do from the New York area, who have either retired here or use these homes as weekend retreats. The Taconic State Parkway, paralleling the Hudson, brings this area within two or three hours' driving time of Manhattan. Few regions can match this westernmost part of New England (and the adjacent strip of New York State east of the Hudson) in its well-groomed rural appearance. North Adams and Pittsfield are two Massachusetts industrial towns. In southwestern Connecticut is Danbury, known for the manufacture of felt hats.

In New York State, the northern uplands continue as the Adirondack Mountains. Here again is a sparsely inhabited region where county populations have either declined or grown very slowly in recent years. Only along the Hudson-Champlain Lowland from Albany north through Lake George and Lake Champlain or in the northwest along the St. Lawrence and Lake Ontario are there sizeable towns. Otherwise, the economy is based largely on tourism, as evidenced by such names as Saranac, Tupper Lake, and Lake Placid. The heavy snowfall makes this an excellent ski area. Much of the region is included within the Adirondack Forest Preserve, a two-and-one-quarter-million-acre state park with numerous campsites and other public facilities.

On the eastern fringe of the Adirondacks are Saratoga Springs, Glens Falls, and Plattsburgh, while to the northwest is Massena, the location of one of the major aluminum-producing plants of the United States. The bauxite for this plant comes from South America and is reduced to alumina in Mobile, Alabama. From there it is taken by rail to northern New York, where plentiful and cheap hydroelectric power is available from the St. Lawrence. Indeed, the opening of the St. Lawrence Seaway in 1959 has been the most hopeful economic move in this northwestern New York area in many decades. With a hydroelectric potential of nearly 2.5 million kilowatts, the seaway has attracted new industries to northern New York, including the Reynolds aluminum plant near Massena and a Chevrolet plant for casting aluminum auto parts. Coupled with this has been the completion of Interstate 81 from Syracuse north through Watertown to Alexandria Bay, thus opening up a relatively isolated area east of Lake Ontario to high-speed auto and truck traffic and to the expansion of an already lucrative tourist trade.

The economic future of the northern uplands might be summed up in two words—tourism and power. Although some of the older tourist spots—such as Bar Harbor, Bretton Woods, and Saratoga Springs—are no longer the fashionable spas of decades ago, the region is close enough to the urban axis to benefit from extensive year-round usage. The creation of new facilities, such as motels, ski tows, and summer camps, plus continued opening up of the area through interstate highways, should prove an ever-increasing economic boom here. There is hope for an eventual reserve of electric power from the St. Lawrence project, as well as from utilization of other sites such as Passamaquoddy or the Allagash River. There is plenty of space in the northern uplands for industrial development. Instead of many small industrial towns, the pattern of the future may be for fewer and much larger industrial complexes.

THE MOHAWK-ONTARIO PLAIN LOWLANDS

From the Albany area westward, the Mohawk Valley extends through the interior highlands to connect with the Ontario Plain and the fringe of lowland along Lake Erie leading to the Midwest. For over 100 miles the broad valley of the Mohawk separates the Adirondacks from the Appalachian Highlands. West of Utica, the Valley broadens out to rolling lowlands. Along this route passed first a rough trail to the west, then, in 1825, the Erie Canal was begun, linking the Hudson with Lake Erie at Buffalo. The canal, over 360 miles long, became a major handler of freight and contributed to the preeminence of New York City as a seaport. By the 1870s, however, the volume of freight moving through the canal was surpassed by that handled on the railroads paralleling the waterway. The various rail lines were eventually consolidated into the New York Central Railroad. Today a main line of the Penn-Central runs from New York City to Albany and then west through Utica and Syracuse to Rochester, Buffalo, and on to the Midwest. The Erie Canal was enlarged and modernized during World War I and now forms the main waterway of the New York State Barge Canal, which has connections with Lake Ontario at Oswego. Thus, through the Mohawk-Ontario Plain corridor now pass the canal, the railroad, and the New York State Thruway.

At the eastern end of the corridor are the three cities of Albany, Troy, and Schenectady, having a total metropolitan population of nearly 800,000. Albany, a commercial center, is also the state capital. Troy, at the head of navigation on the Hudson and at the outlet of the State Barge Canal, is an old industrial city, specializing in shirts and machinery. Schenectady, northwest of Albany on the Mohawk River, is the home of General Electric and of American Locomotive works. This urban complex is in economic difficulties, with declining manufactures and an out-migration of 38 percent of the population of the central cities between 1960 and 1970. Albany's ambitious urban-renewal program represents a brave effort to reverse the trend, but this state administration program is one of the few hopeful activities taking place in this area.

To the west along the Mohawk Valley are Amsterdam, Utica, and Rome—industrial cities that have specialized in textiles, carpets, metals, and machinery. Economically, this region is much like eastern and southern New England, and the cities have been in a steady industrial decline during recent decades. At Rome, where the city is undergoing a $33 million renewal program, a 1974 decision by the Defense Department to close nearby Griffiss Air Force Base came as a shattering blow. The closure will eliminate up to 14,000 military and civilian jobs and have an estimated $100 million annual impact on central New York State.

In the Rome area, the hills gradually merge into the Ontario Plain. Syracuse, fifty miles west of Rome, is the first of the three major western New York cities. With a population of 215,000, it is located near important salt deposits and is noted for soda ash, in which salt is mixed with coal and local limestone. The Solvay Company, a producer of soda ash, is one of the largest industries in Syracuse.

The city grew up during the nineteenth century on the Erie Canal at the junction with the Oswego Canal, a canal running north to Lake Ontario. Later it became an important railroad junction, and now is a highway center at the intersection of the New York State Thruway and Interstate 81, which runs from Philadelphia north through Watertown. Unlike the cities to the east, Syracuse has adjusted well to postwar economic conditions and is a thriving industrial area.

Eighty miles to the west of Syracuse is Rochester, on Lake Ontario, a city of 300,000 people; it produces cameras, electrical machinery, optical equipment, and other technical products and is the home of Eastman Kodak and Bausch and Lomb optical works. Rochester is set in an intensively developed agricultural region that takes advantage of the ameliorating effects of the nearby water. Along the southern and eastern shores of Lake Ontario is a major fruit belt, producing apples, grapes, peaches, cherries, and pears, as well as vegetables and sugar beets. Four counties along the south shore of the lake produced, between them, agricultural products worth $82 million in 1969. Food processing is an important industry in many of the towns of this flat, western New York area.

Economic developments in the area are uneven. A Japanese trading company is constructing a steel mill in Auburn, southwest of Syracuse, with a yearly capacity of 150,000 tons. Built on a 200-acre site, the plant will provide employment for 250 persons in a town that lost 2,000 jobs in 1948, when International Harvester closed its farm machinery plant, and 900 more when the Firth Carpet Company went out of business. Twenty-five miles northeast of Auburn, the new town of Raddison is being constructed by the Urban Development Corporation, designed eventually to have a population of 18,000. Raddison will be the site of a Schlitz Brewing Company plant,

employing 600, and of the regional headquarters of the State
Farm Insurance Company, employing 1,000.

But ninety miles to the west of Raddison, another new town
has foundered. Riverton, a community of 1,000 located near
Rochester, has failed in its efforts to gain new financing from
commercial banks. Begun with funds from the Department of
Housing and Urban Development, it was one of a series of new
towns financed primarily from the sale of federally guaranteed
bonds. The town was built on a 2,500-acre site and was designed to attract 25,000 people and 11,000 jobs. About a third
of the proposed dwellings were to be earmarked for low- and
moderate-income families. Although more than $16 million
was invested in Riverton, inflation and the problems besetting
the homebuilding industry combined to obstruct the sale of
new homes and the attraction of new industries to the community.

In extreme western New York is the Niagara Frontier, containing Buffalo and Niagara Falls. Power for this area is supplied by the Falls, and in the city of Niagara Falls are important
chemical plants, as well as metal and paper industries. Buffalo
profits from its location; it is at the end of Lake Erie, yet close
to the coal fields of Pennsylvania. Iron ore is brought by ship
to Bethlehem Steel's great Lackawanna plant, south of the city.
Coal is imported by rail from the south, while limestone is
quarried in the vicinity of Buffalo. The city has also been a
major flour-milling center; the flour is brought to the port by
ship from the west. Automobiles and automobile parts are
brought by water to Buffalo, there to be transferred for ship-
ment by truck or rail to New York and New England. There
is also a Chevrolet assembly plant and a Ford stamping plant
in Buffalo, as well as the Bell aircraft factory.

But Buffalo in recent years has been experiencing financial
difficulties. Steel production has declined, ships have begun
to bypass the port, carrying their cargoes directly to the ocean
via the St. Lawrence Seaway, and railroad service has dropped
considerably. Between 1960 and 1970, the city's population
dropped 11 percent, leaving the municipal government in seri-

ous difficulty with regard to providing essential services for the city. Despite its location and its excellent rail, highway, and water connections, Buffalo is an old city in need of extensive renewal and economic rehabilitation. Its hinterland is not a particularly viable one, and many of the services that it has traditionally performed can also be taken care of just as efficiently in other areas.

One problem of the Mohawk-Ontario Plain area is that it lacks a regional capital. Buffalo, Rochester, Syracuse, and the eastern cities are strung out in a line as separate units removed from major population agglomerations. Railways and highways link them with the urban axis and the Midwest, and cheap and plentiful electric power is being developed for the area, but these advantages alone are not enough to ensure future growth. This upstate New York area has few economic advantages that are not also present in other parts of the United States.

Southwest of Buffalo, a narrow lowland route extends westward along the southern shore of Lake Erie, bordering the Appalachian Highlands, into Pennsylvania and Ohio. The major city here is Erie, Pennsylvania, with 130,000 people. It is an important harbor for the export of coal from the Pittsburgh area and the import of iron ore, grain, and petroleum. Along this lowland corridor runs the Penn-Central Railroad to Cleveland, as well as Interstate 90 to connect with the midwestern highway net.

THE APPALACHIAN HIGHLANDS

South of the Mohawk-Ontario Plain lowlands, the Appalachians extend through southernmost New York, Pennsylvania, northwestern New Jersey, and western Maryland. Most of the region is a maturely dissected upland, with many ridges, low mountains, and elongated valleys. In western Pennsylvania, the landscape is extremely rugged, with few natural transportation routes across it. Much of the Highlands is included in northern Appalachia, an area of considerable concern because of the widespread conditions of poverty that exist there.

Winters tend to be long, and precipitation heavy. Soils are generally poor, and most of the area is marginal agriculturally, except in dairying areas where transportation to urban markets is feasible. Pennsylvania has extensive coal deposits, and there is some petroleum and natural gas here and in southwestern New York State, as well as limestone, slate, and timber. But the demand for the area's natural resources has been dropping since the early years of the twentieth century, and many of the problems endemic to the northern uplands are also present here. Recreation and new industries seem to offer the principal economic hope for the future.

The Appalachian Highlands will be considered in terms of two subdivisions: the Delaware-Susquehanna area in the east, and the Allegheny Plateau in the west. The boundary between these is the Allegheny Front, a 2,000-foot escarpment in western Pennsylvania.

The Eastern Highlands

In southeastern New York State, the edge of the Greater New York City area is marked by a ridge of hills extending southwest from Bear Mountain on the Hudson across New Jersey to the Allentown-Bethlehem area of Pennsylvania. West of this ridge is the fertile Walkill Valley, where dairying is an important activity, and beyond are the beginnings of the Catskill Mountains. Dairying is also carried on in the Catskills, but the region is far more important for tourism, particularly in such Sullivan County resorts as Monticello, Liberty, and Livingston Manor,

West of the Catskills are the hills of south-central New York State, drained by the upper Susquehanna. From Cooperstown west through the Finger Lakes is an area of dairying, general farming, and the raising of apples and grapes. It is a pleasant region with towns growing slowly, if at all. In the south, close to the Pennsylvania border, are the Triple Cities—Binghamton, Johnson City, and Endicott—spread out along the Susquehanna. Except for Pittsburgh, this is the largest urban area in the Appalachian Highlands. The Triple Cities are best known as the original home of International Business Machines and the Endicott-Johnson Shoe Company, and the population of 300,000 continues to grow at a fairly rapid rate. The urban core has good rail and highway connections and has become a focal point for a large area in southern New York and northern Pennsylvania. The Susquehanna system extends west of the Triple Cities to include the Chemung Valley, with its historic towns of Elmira, Hornell, and Corning (with its famous glass works).

Downstream on the Susquehanna, in the Wyoming Valley, are Scranton and Wilkes-Barre, an area of significant population decline. From here and from some 30 miles to the south, near Hazleton, come practically all the anthracite coal produced in the United States. Anthracite was first used for blacksmithing in the mid-eighteenth century. Up until the 1870s, the bulk of the American iron industry was located in eastern Pennsylvania, utilizing its hard coal and iron-ore resources. The introduction of coke processes and the discovery of greater ore resources in the Midwest eventually ended Pennsylvania's predominance, but anthracite production continued to grow because of its use in domestic heating. The peak was reached just prior to World War I; since then anthracite production has been on a gradual decline. During World War II there was a modest increase in output to about 60 million tons per year, but by 1971 production was down to less than one-sixth of that figure.

What happens to a region of over a million people as their main economic livelihood gradually slips away? For one thing, the inhabitants leave. Between 1950 and 1970 three anthracite counties—Lackawanna, Lucerne, and Schuylkill—each suffered a loss in population. There is little agriculture in this rugged area of Pennsylvania; the natural move would then be to attract industry. But the region is relatively isolated and without a large pool of skilled or semiskilled labor. Some textile and clothing plants have been established in the Scranton-Wilkes-Barre area, but these employ mostly women at low wages. Silk, lace, shoes, and mining machinery are other products manufactured here.

The Wyoming Valley was the scene of Hurricane "Agnes" in 1972. During this hurricane, the Susquehanna River flooded much of downtown Wilkes-Barre, forcing 100,000 residents from their homes. In the weeks following the flood, community leaders urged the federal government to acquire flood-damaged homes at the preflood market value, thereby enabling residents to start over again in safer locations. Many people in the business community opposed relocation, and in the end, the government decided to make available low-interest loans, enabling residents to fix up their waterlogged homes. As a result, much of the low-lying areas are back to normal: the homes gradually being repaired and repainted; the homeowners saddled with thirty-year mortgages; and the city still vulnerable to another devastating flood. Meanwhile, federal funding has also made possible a $200 million downtown project, including shopping malls, office space, and parking facilities, located a block away from the banks of the Susquehanna.

Southwest of the anthracite area is Harrisburg, a rail and highway center just below the juncture of the Susquehanna and Juniata rivers. The latter, coming in from the west, provides a major lowland route through the Folded Appalachians and is followed by the Penn-Central Railroad. Harrisburg, a city of 70,000, serves as the state capital and is also the site of a small steel mill. The Pennsylvania Turnpike crosses the north-south Susquehanna Valley here; and from Harrisburg, highways radiate out to Gettysburg and York in the south and to Lancaster, Reading, and Allentown to the east. Each of these towns is a regional center of some importance.

The physical geography of southeastern Pennsylvania is complicated by its variety of physiographic regions. To the west are the rugged Appalachian Highlands. These end in a prominent ridge on the southeast called the Shawangunks in New York State, Kittatinny in New Jersey, and Blue Mountain in Pennsylvania. This ridge overlooks the Great Valley, a series of structural lowlands extending northeast-southwest from the Hudson lowland across New Jersey and Pennsylvania. Much of the Great Valley is underlain with limestone, providing the basis for good soil. Southeast of the Great Valley is a hilly area, far less rugged than the Appalachian area to the north. This region, the Piedmont, contains broad valleys and several areas of excellent soil, particularly around Lancaster and York.

Across southeastern Pennsylvania flow four rivers at right angles to the physiographic regions. In the north is the Delaware River, which cuts through the Kittatinny ridge in the Delaware Water Gap at Stroudsburg and then flows past Philadelphia to the sea. Below this is the Lehigh River, rising in the Appalachian Highlands near Scranton; the river cuts through Blue Mountain near Allentown and then turns east to join the Delaware above Trenton. Along the lower Lehigh are the cities of Allentown, Bethlehem, and Easton. Farther south is the Schuylkill, which also comes from the north to cut through the ridge across the Great Valley past Reading and then wend its way through the Piedmont to the Delaware at Philadelphia. Finally there is the Susquehanna, which breaks through Blue Mountain at Harrisburg and then flows down to Chesapeake Bay. During the nineteenth century, the Delaware, Lehigh, and Schuylkill rivers were made navigable by a series of canals. Later these were superseded by railroads focusing on Philadelphia.

Allentown, northernmost of the cities considered here, is an industrial center on the Lehigh River shortly below its break through Blue Mountain. Its principal industry is cement, based on local limestone deposits. It also has a history of iron and steel works and is surrounded by fertile farmland. Downstream on the Lehigh is Bethlehem, the home of the Bethlehem Steel Company and the site of one of the larger steel mills in the East. These cities, together with Easton (a few miles to the east at the juncture of the Lehigh and Delaware rivers) owe their early rise to local iron ores and the proximity of anthracite coal 50 miles away in Scranton, and also to the nineteenth-century canal system that linked them with Philadelphia. Many manufactures based on the early iron and steel industries still remain in the Lehigh Valley and contribute to its economic position.

Southwest of Allentown is Reading, on the Schuylkill River 60 miles from Philadelphia. Reading was an early producer of iron and steel, but more recently it has become a hosiery center and textile town. It also adjoins a rich agricultural region. Still farther to the southwest is Lancaster, on the Conestoga River, which flows west to the Susquehanna. The region around Lancaster is one of the most intensively farmed in the United States. It is an area of gently rolling hills, with extremely fertile limestone soil. The farmers are mostly of German stock and maintain relatively small, well-kept farms that specialize in tobacco, potatoes, and grain. Here, and in the surrounding areas, is the center of the nation's mushroom production—a specialty of the excellent soils and scientific farming methods. This region is also the center for the old-order Amish Mennonites, a religious sect that may be identified by its somber clothes and its horse-and-buggy transport.

West of Lancaster and across the Susquehanna is York, also an agricultural and manufacturing center. Thirty miles beyond York is Gettysburg, another rich agricultural town and scene of the famous battlefield. Just west of Gettysburg is the northernmost extension of the Blue Ridge. It was behind these mountains that General Lee moved northward through the Great Valley to Chambersburg during the Civil War, where he turned east through the Blue Ridge to Gettysburg and the Union army.

Practically all these southeastern Pennsylvania cities have in common their highly productive farming hinterland, a diversified manufacturing base, and the advantages of good communications with Philadelphia, Baltimore, and Washington. They are well served by railroads, and in recent years, by turnpikes. The terrain may be gently rolling or hilly, but it is never as rugged as that north of Harrisburg or Stroudsburg. This is a pleasant and accessible group of cities and towns. It is close enough to the urban axis to contain the weekend or summer retreats of the well-to-do, some of whom buy old Pennsylvania Dutch homes and become part-time gentlemen farmers. To the south, this region extends across Maryland, west of the Baltimore-Washington area. Frederick and Hagerstown are the two urban centers here, both of them important for farming.

The Great Valley is the easternmost part of the Folded Appalachians, a seemingly endless series of ridges and valleys trending in a general northeast-southwest direction. The ridges, representing sandstone and other resistant rocks, are generally wooded; while the valleys are often farmed, although most of this is a marginal agricultural area. Three rivers cross the Folded Appalachians from west to east: the west branch of the Susquehanna in the north; the Juniata in south-central Pennsylvania; and the Potomac along the southern border of Maryland.

There are no cities of over 50,000 in the Folded Appalachians, except for the anthracite towns of Scranton and Wilkes-Barre; rather, there are regional centers for agriculture or small manufacturing. Dairying, general farming, sheep raising, and lumbering are the major economic activities, along with some manufacturing and tourism. In the north, along the valley of the west branch of the Susquehanna, are the towns of Lewisburg, Williamsport, and Lockport. The valley is followed by a branch of the Penn-Central Railroad linking Philadelphia with Buffalo. The area's relative isolation ended with the construction of the 313-mile Interstate 80—the Keystone Shortway across central Pennsylvania from Stroudsburg to Sharon, Ohio, near Youngstown. This provides the shortest turnpike route between New York and Chicago. The highway passes south of Williamsport and Lock Haven. It parallels the Pennsylvania Turnpike 60 miles to the south and has opened up northern Pennsylvania both to tourism and to industry.

The Juniata River, which joins with the Susquehanna just above Harrisburg, is paralleled by the main line of the Penn-Central Railroad. Lewistown is the only important town on the river. North of the Juniata, in the Nittany Valley, is University Park, home of Pennsylvania State University. South of the Juniata, there are no important regional centers until one reaches Cumberland, Maryland, a town of 40,000, where nearby coal deposits give rise to a small iron and steel industry.

Cumberland, on the Potomac, is located at a gap in the mountains that leads westward to the Ohio River system. Through this gap passes the main line of the Baltimore & Ohio Railroad into West Virginia.

The Allegheny Plateau

In south-central Pennsylvania is the Allegheny Front, a rim nearly 2,000 feet in height that curves northeast to southwest, from Williamsport down into Maryland. The Allegheny Front marks the eastern end of the Allegheny Plateau, a region of nearly horizontal rock strata, which contains the bulk of the nation's bituminous coal deposits. The Plateau is deeply dissected by the Allegheny River and its tributaries, and in the southwest, by the Monongahela, which flows north from West Virginia to join the Allegheny at Pittsburgh and form the Ohio River.

Coal is the principal resource of the Plateau. Although forests abound, most of them have been cut over, and there has been little effort at management of the second growth. In the northern, glaciated area, there is some dairying and general farming; but in the central and southern sectors, agriculture is very limited. One of the important potentials of the Plateau area is tourism. The Allegheny National Forest in northwestern Pennsylvania serves as an attraction for people from both the Pittsburgh and Buffalo areas. In extreme northwestern Pennsylvania are a number of lakes and reservoirs that are accessible to vacationists from Pittsburgh, Erie, and the northeastern Ohio cities.

A northern extension of the Allegheny Plateau includes the southern New York towns of Jamestown, Olean, and Wellsville, the latter an oil-refining center. Southwestern New York State is largely a dairying area, except around Lake Chautauqua, west of Jamestown, where grapes are important.

The coal industry of the Allegheny Plateau is concentrated for the most part in the rugged southwestern area. There streams have eaten down into the upland, exposing coal seams that can be mined horizontally from the valley sides. Practically all the mines are now mechanized, and a growing proportion of the coal is being obtained by strip mining. This process involves removing the overburden of soil and rock and then exploiting the nearly horizontal seams.

The soft coal industry in Pennsylvania underwent a considerable decline both in production and employment in the years after World War I. The nine principal coal-producing counties (excluding Allegheny County, in which Pittsburgh is located) have among them a population of 1.5 million. This region suffered a net out-migration of 63,000 people between 1960 and 1970.

The state of Pennsylvania lost its traditional lead in coal mining to West Virginia before World War II; now it is in third place, behind that state and Kentucky. Within Pennsylvania itself there has been a marked difference between the southwestern counties (in which the bulk of the coal is mined), where production continues to decline, and the north-central and west-central counties, where strip mining is far more important and where production in recent years has been rising. The soft coal industry has hopes of maintaining and even improving its competitive position (so far as production is concerned), although its labor demand will probably continue to decline. One of the major coal costs is that of transportation. In recent years this cost has been declining because of the use of long, unitized trains and of faster turn-around operations of coal cars. Coal still supplies about 45 percent of the energy requirements of the nation's utility companies, and coal executives are banking on a continually rising demand for electricity in the United States to keep up the market for coal. This forecast has been bolstered by the recent increase in oil prices. Project Independence, which would seek to make the nation virtually self-sufficient in energy requirements, should certainly cause a major upward revision of coal production in the Appalachians. From a 1974 figure of approximately 600 million tons production, estimates call for a figure of 1.5 to 2 billion tons by 1985. The 1.5 billion figure would mean the opening of new mines, requiring an investment in the coal industry of $16 billion, and an increase in employment from the current 150,000 miners to about 200,000. From all this, southwestern Pennsylvania would surely stand to benefit.

Industries based on coal, local clay and sand resources, and the availability of iron ore from the Great Lakes ports are spread across western and southwestern Pennsylvania. Altoona, at the foot of the Allegheny Front, is an important railroad town for both maintenance and the production of rail equipment. Johnstown, forty miles to the west, produces iron and steel, cement, and clay products. In 1889, it was the scene of a disastrous flood, in which over 2,200 persons lost their lives when a dam burst on the Conemaugh River. Other western Pennsylvania towns with heavy industry are New Castle, New Kensington, and Oil City. All depend on the availability of iron ore, coal, and limestone and are strongly oriented toward the iron and steel industry, either in the primary producing phase or in fabrication of iron and steel products.

The giant, of course, is Pittsburgh, twenty-fourth city of the United States and sixth largest in the Northeast. The Standard Metropolitan Area includes Allegheny and three adjacent counties, with a total of 2.4 million people, three-quarters of them outside the limits of the city of Pittsburgh.

The focus of Pittsburgh is the Golden Triangle, a triangular area at the junction of the Allegheny and Monongahela rivers. Both are navigable for some distance upstream from Pittsburgh for vessels drawing up to nine feet. On the Monongahela, in particular, coal may be brought by barge from the Pennsylvania or West Virginia mines. Petroleum products, sand and gravel, or other bulk goods can move up the Ohio toward Pittsburgh, while iron ore arrives by rail from Cleveland or other Lake Erie ports just over 100 miles away. About 15 percent of the nation's steel-making capacity is located in Pittsburgh or in nearby river towns such as Donora and Monessen on the Monongahela or Midland on the Ohio below the Golden Triangle.

Pittsburgh was the home of Andrew Carnegie, the giant of the steel industry 80 years ago. In the area are large plants of

U.S. Steel and also of Jones & Laughlin, a Pittsburgh steel concern. On the basis of the city's early prominence in iron and steel, a great number of metal-fabricating plants have grown up nearby, producing everything from turbines and generators to complex machine tools. Unfortunately for the Pittsburgh area, the effect of technological change in the steel industry has been to reduce the differentials in the cost of basic materials, making the industry increasingly market oriented. Much of the expansion in steel, therefore, has taken place either along the East Coast or in the Midwest. To compensate, the plants in the Pittsburgh area have had to introduce modern labor-saving machinery, thus cutting down the number of employees in the local steel concerns.

Pittsburgh was the nation's leading glass-making center in the nineteenth century, but its relative position has declined considerably. In the fifteen years following World War II, employment in its glass industry dropped by one-third. Similarly, the electrical machinery industry, which received such an initial impetus from the work of Pittsburgh's George Westinghouse, has undergone nationwide dispersion. One of this area's problems is that most of its industrial specialties are industries in which national employment in recent years has been declining or growing very slowly. Unlike the other major urban areas of the Northeast, the Pittsburgh area has experienced relatively little influx of new types of industry. Another problem is the high proportion of unskilled or semiskilled workers—a condition that authorities in the area are trying rapidly to change through education and retraining programs. But even with the opening of the Pennsylvania Turnpike and Interstate 70 from Erie through Pittsburgh to West Virginia and south, the city remains in a somewhat isolated position with respect to both the East Coast and the Midwest. As its locational advantages for steel, coal, glass, and other heavy industries decline relative to those of other parts of the United States, Pittsburgh is forced to compensate through technological innovations or the development of new sources of income.

Despite its economic problems, the city was one of the first in the United States to inaugurate a comprehensive redevelopment program after World War II. Actually, the city's *renaissance* began in 1944 and has now burgeoned into an ongoing operation. The ban on smoke, first legislated in 1947, has been extended to cover all of Allegheny County. The Golden Triangle, once a city slum, is now a state park adjoining the Gateway Center project. There are new skyscrapers, new parkways, a new $100 million sewage-disposal project covering Allegheny County, a public auditorium, and a projected $250 million Panther Hollow research park. No other city of its size in the Northeast has (through the use of both public and private funds) made such headway in redevelopment and renewal as has the city of Pittsburgh.

But in the midst of this urban improvement is the general economic condition of western Pennsylvania, particularly the rural areas and the old industrial towns. In 1960, governors from eleven states in the Appalachian area met to discuss their mutual economic problems. Three years later, President Kennedy established an Appalachian Regional Commission for a 165,000-square-mile area, stretching from the Pennsylvania-New York border south through northern Alabama. In Pennsylvania, Appalachia includes all but the southeastern part of the state; in Maryland it lies to the west of Frederick. Although there are pockets of relative prosperity in Appalachia, the region in general is one of economic depression.

In 1965, Congress passed the Appalachian Redevelopment Act. It created the Appalachian Regional Commission to design and develop comprehensive plans and programs for Appalachia. The bill, as amended, provided nearly $1.8 billion for the region, two-thirds of which was allocated to the construction of some 2,700 miles of highways intended to link with the interstate system and to open up isolated areas to settlement, industry, and tourism. In Pennsylvania, most of the road building has been in the south-central area, from University Park, Altoona, and Johnstown south to the Maryland border. A new road in Maryland also parallels the state border from Hagerstown west through Cumberland, while to the north, in southwestern New York State, Route 17 is being improved westward from Elmira. But it has been argued that there has been in fact no coordinated regional plan, and that local benefits have taken priority over regional objectives. The road-building program is in a sense unique in the United States as an effort to open up for economic development an economically depressed area. As in the case of the Tennessee Valley Authority—a much more ambitious regional development program—it may take years before the true impact of the road building and other programs in Appalachia can be fully realized.

6 The Northeast in Perspective

The Northeast has been shown here to be a region of tradition and change, a region with many problems, but one that, in the past, has shown itself capable of grappling with the complexities of changing times and of retaining its position of preeminence in the United States. In summary, let us look briefly at some of the basic problems now facing the Northeast and at the steps that are or may be taken to remedy them.

In Chapter 2, some of the major difficulties faced by the larger urban areas were discussed. A few of these are relevant to other sectors of the Northeast as well. First, there is the *competition for space* in economically valuable areas—whether these areas be in or near cities, along fresh- or saltwater shorelines, or in fertile agricultural areas, such as parts of the Great Valley. The competition arises from the conflict between varying types of use to be adopted in these areas. One type of solution to this conflict lies in adequate zoning regulations; another comes through long-range planning to ensure that, over the years, maximum utilization be made of the space. Such planning is also necessary for future parks and other recreation sites and for reservoirs, airports, and other major consumers of space on the periphery of densely crowded areas. The Northeast is well endowed with professional planners, but tradition frequently tends to weigh against adequate zoning laws and truly effective long-range planning.

A second problem is that of *obsolescence*—whether it be of urban areas, farms, mines, or industries. Because of its long history of settlement and economic development, the Northeast of today has inherited many things from the past that the present population is reluctant to eliminate or change. Bulldozers may level parts of the cities' central business districts or specially selected slum areas, but such activities only scratch the surface of the basic urban problems. Most city dwellers remain unaffected by these dramatic moves. The same is true in farming and mining and in many of the industries that one way or another manage to hang on from year to year. Must such economic activities eventually be eliminated completely, or are there aspects that could be retained together with innovations? Here is a challenge that in some fields is being successfully met: in the construction of electric power stations at the entrances of coal mines, in the agricultural specialization in farms of the Great Valley, and in the move toward industrial change-over in the cities of southeastern New England.

A third problem is that of *movement.* The large and relatively affluent population of the Northeast is highly mobile, not only within the cities but also between cities and in rural areas. The decline of the railroads, the need for mass transit in urban regions (and the perference by many travelers for private automobiles), the inadequacies of airports, and the isolation of many nonurban parts of the Northeast—these and similar difficulties require long-range solutions. It is to the credit of the state and local governments here, as well as of the federal government itself, that many of the problems of movement are being faced squarely and, at considerable expense, are being remedied. But mobility is a constantly growing phenomenon that will require frequent attention and increasingly large expenditures of funds.

Finally there is the problem of the *people* themselves—of their ability to live together in close proximity to one another and to face the changing economic, social, and political conditions of the Northeast. Can they adjust to the continued influx of differing ethnic groups? Can they cope with the social problems of mass migration from the cities and the farms to the suburbs, and for some, from the suburbs back to the cities again? Can they elect to the various governing bodies the people who can best cope with the complex problems of the area? Will they support the decisions of their governments or seek to circumvent them? Here in the political realm is perhaps the most basic problem of all; for only through wise leadership can the Northeast hope to retain at least some of its former stature.

In conclusion, let us look at a few of the trends now discernible in the Northeast and, through them, try to assess something of the region's future development. First, consider population. As noted in Chapter 1, the Northeast's share of the national population has been declining every decade since World War I. This is likely to continue, at least for the foreseeable future, together with continued out-migration of whites and an influx into the urban areas of blacks and Puerto Ricans. The exodus of middle-income groups from the cities to the suburbs will also continue, but at a declining rate. The newer suburbs, for some of the cities, are growing further and further away from the urban centers; the choked highways and rising gas prices make commuting by automobile less attractive; the costs of homes and services in some suburbs are almost prohibitive. People accustomed to city living may elect to remain there or move back to the urban areas rather than cope with suburban problems.

At the same time, the growing suburban sprawl between southern Maine and northern Virginia may also decelerate. The tendency for towns and bedroom communities to grow closer toward one another along metropolitan axes has existed for the past two decades, but again, rising costs and the energy crisis will affect this. The failure of some new towns to reach conditions of takeoff, and the bankruptcy of planned residential-recreational communities may halt or at least slow down the absorption of vacant land in the populous parts of the Northeast for housing and commercial developments. The trend away from expansion of developments is only beginning, but it is expected to continue at least through the rest of the decade.

One limiting factor to growth in the Northeast is the high price of commodities; energy is one example. In 1974, oil supplied 46 percent of the nation's energy needs, but 85 percent of the energy requirements of New England. And the bulk of New England's oil is imported from overseas. Food, building materials, chemicals—items such as these have traditionally been more expensive in the Northeast than in most other parts of the nation.

There will be a continued decline in the number of people in the Northeast in commercial agriculture, both in farms on the urban fringe and those in more rural areas. The concentration of employment, capital, and technical innovations in agriculture is a continuing trend. Similarly, there will be a decrease or, at best, a leveling off in the number of persons employed in the extractive industries—mining, quarrying, lumbering, and fishing—in the Northeast. So far as the smaller cities are concerned, the pattern of future growth will continue to be uneven. Many will for some years continue their gradual economic decline until their population level reaches an equilibrium with their economic development. New Bedford, Portland, Utica, Scranton, and Altoona are representative of this group. On the other hand, some cities will benefit, either from new industries or from special power or other developments nearby. Cities that may show economic growth in the coming years are: Binghamton, the hub of interstate highway systems; Massena, because of hydroelectric developments; and Wilmington, if a new superport is built in Delaware Bay.

The continued shift away from primary occupations in the Northeast is paralleled to some extent by the gradual decline in secondary or manufacturing occupations as well. Industries requiring considerable technical skill will no doubt hold their own. But except for particular areas, such as the Hackensack

Meadowlands, the Delaware Valley, and eastern Baltimore, heavy industry seems destined to be increasingly less important in the economy of the Northeast.

But there will be a steady increase in the tertiary occupations—that is, those that service either production and processing industries or the consumer himself. Gottmann has even suggested that there be a differentiation between tertiary and quaternary industries. The former involve "transportation, trade, in the simpler sense of direct sales, maintenance, and personal services." The latter include "services that involve transactions, analysis, research, or decision making, and also education and government."[5] Quaternary services require more intellectual training and responsibility than do the tertiary ones, but the Northeast, as a center for commerce, communications, education and research, and government activities, can afford to expand in both service types.

Another future trend involves the role of the federal government, and particularly of federal funds, in the Northeast. Consider, for example, the nature of federal assistance in urban renewal, a task particularly necessary for the old industrial cities in this part of the nation. There are defense funds on which certain areas have been uniquely dependent; directly, as in the case of the military bases near Portsmouth or Newport; or indirectly, as in the aircraft and submarine industries of Connecticut or electronics in Massachusetts. The federal hand is evident in the St. Lawrence Seaway project, the interstate highway system, and the funds for Appalachia. It dominates the city of Washington and is enjoined to help save Amtrak. In short, the federal role in the Northeast is a unique one; no other section of the United States with comparable population is so dependent upon funds from Washington.

In order to survive, such an economy must be in close symbiosis with the rest of the nation. The Northeast must avoid

5. Ibid., p. 576.

becoming isolated as capital and markets move toward the west and south. It must also avoid duplications of its specialized functions in other parts of the United States, or it will lose its vital role in the nation's economic and political life. The retention of its dominant position, particularly in specialized manufactures and services, depends on wise planning and investment, on acceptance of innovations, and on coordinated action by the region's various public and private agencies. If its dominant role is retained, the Northeast will continue to be an extremely enjoyable place in which to live and work and a vital force in the nation's future development.

Suggested Readings

Books

Brown, Ralph H. *Historical Geography of the United States.* New York: Harcourt Brace Jovanovich, 1948.

───── *Mirror for Americans: Likeness of the Eastern Seaboard, 1810.* New York: American Geographical Society, 1943.

Census of Agriculture, 1969. Washington, D.C.: U.S. Government Printing Office, 1972.

Census of Population, 1970: Characteristics of the Population. Washington, D.C.: U.S. Government Printing Office, 1972.

County and City Data Book, 1972. Washington, D.C.: U.S. Government Printing Office, 1973.

Dansereau, Pierre, ed. *Challenge for Survival: Land, Air and Water for Man in Megalopolis.* New York: Columbia University Press, 1970.

Estall, Robert. *A Modern Geography of the United States.* Baltimore: Penguin Books, 1970.

───── . *New England: A Study of Industrial Adjustment.* New York: Praeger, 1966.

Fenneman, N. M. *Physiography of the Eastern United States.* New York: McGraw-Hill, 1930.

Fisheries of the United States, 1973. Washington, D.C.: U.S. Government Printing Office, 1974.

Gottmann, Jean. *Megalopolis: The Urbanized Northeastern Seaboard of the United States.* New York: The Twentieth Century Fund, 1961.

───── . "Urbanization and the American Landscape." In *Problems and Trends in American Geography,* ed. Saul B. Cohen. New York: Basic Books, 1968.

Gottman, Jean, and Robert A. Harper, eds. *Megalopolis on the Move: Geographers Look at Urban Sprawl.* New York: Wiley, 1967.

Kantrowitz, Nathan. *Negro and Puerto Rican Populations of New York City in the Twentieth Century.* American Geographical Society Studies in Urban Geography, No. 1. New York: American Geographical Society, 1969.

New England's Prospect, 1933. American Geographical Society Special Publication, No. 16. New York: American Geographical Society, 1933.

Paterson, J. H. *North America: A Geography of Canada and the United States.* New York: Oxford University Press, 1970.

Thompson, John H., ed. *Geography of New York State.* Syracuse, N.Y.: Syracuse University Press, 1966.

Visher, Stephen S. *Climatic Atlas of the United States.* Cambridge, Mass.: Harvard University Press, 1954.

White, C. Langdon, Edwin J. Foscue, and Tom L. McKnight. *Regional Geography of Anglo-America.* 4th ed. Englewood Cliffs, N. J.: Prentice-Hall, 1974.

Ward, David. *Cities and Immigrants.* New York: Oxford University Press, 1971.

Yeates, Maurice H., and Barry F. Gerner. *The North American City.* New York: Harper & Row, 1971.

Articles

Borchert, J. R. "American Metropolitan Evolution." *Geographical Review* 57 (1967): 301–32.

_____. "America's Changing Metropolitan Regions." *Annals of the Association of American Geographers* 62 (1972): 352–74.

Brodsky, Harold. "Land Development and the Expanding City." *Annals of the Association of American Geographers* 63 (1973): 159–67.

Carey, George W., Leonore Macomber, and Michael Greenberg. "Educational and Demographic Factors in the Urban Geography of Washington, D.C." *Geographical Review* 58 (1968): 515–38.

Cutler, Irving. "Megalopolis: Intermetropolitan Coalescence." *Journal of Geography* 68 (1969): 454–64.

Deasey, George F., and Phyllis R. Griess. "Local and Regional Differences in Long Term Bituminous Coal Production in Eastern United States." *Annals of the Association of American Geographers* 57 (1967): 519–33.

Durand, Loyal, Jr. "The Historical and Economic Geography of Dairying in the North County of New York State." *Geographical Review* 57 (1967): 24–47.

_____. "The Major Milksheds of the Northeastern Quarter of the United States." *Economic Geography* 40 (1964): 9–34.

Fillmore, C. Earney. "Mushrooms and Mines: A Study in Horticulture." *Journal of Geography* 67 (1968): 42–48.

_____. "New Ores for Old Furnaces: Pelletized Iron." *Annals of the Association of American Geographers* 59 (1969): 512–39.

_____. "Vermont's Mineral Industries." *Journal of Geography* 66 (1967): 63–69.

Gauthier, Howard L. "The Appalachian Development Highway System: Development for Whom?" *Economic Geography* 49 (1973): 103–09.

Greenberg, Michael R., George W. Carey, Leonard Zobler, and Robert M. Hordon. "A Geographical Systems Analysis of the Water Supply Networks of the New York Metropolitan Region." *Geographical Review* 61 (1971): 339–55.

Gregor, Howard F. "Farm Structures in Regional Comparison: California and New Jersey Vegetable Farms." *Economic Geography* 45 (1969): 209–26.

Hart, John Fraser. "Loss and Abandonment of Cleared Farm Land in the Eastern United States." *Annals of the Association of American Geographers* 58 (1968): 417–41.

Hartshorn, Truman A. "Inner City Residential Structure and Decline." *Annals of the Association of American Geographers* 61 (1971): 72–96.

Higbee, Edward. "The Three Earths of New England." *Geographical Review* 42 (1952): 425–38.

Holmes, John H. "Linkages Between External Communities and Out-Migration: Evidence from Middle-Eastern Pennsylvania." *Economic Geography* 48 (1972): 406–21.

Klimm, Lester E. "The Empty Areas of the Northeastern United States." *Geographical Review* 44 (1954): 325–45.

Landing, James E. "The Amish, the Automobile, and Social Interaction." *Journal of Geography* 71 (1972): 52–57.

Lewis, George K. "Population Change in Northern New England." *Annals of the Association of American Geographers* 62 (1972): 307–23.

Lewis, Peirce F. "Small Town in Pennsylvania." *Annals of the Association of American Geographers* 62 (1972): 323–52.

Lewis, Thomas R. "Recent Changes in the Connecticut Valley Tobacco Industry." *Journal of Geography* 68 (1969): 46–49.

Mason, Peter F. "Some Changes in Domestic Iron Mining as a Result of Pelletization." *Annals of the Association of American Geographers* 59 (1969): 535–52.

Patton, Donald J. "General Cargo Hinterlands of New York, Philadelphia, Baltimore, and New Orleans." *Annals of the Association of American Geographers* 48 (1958): 436–56.

Van Burkalow, Anastasia. "The Geography of New York City's Water Supply: A Study of Interactions." *Geographical Review* 49 (1959): 369–86.

Wallace, William H. "The Future of the Freight Train in New England." *Proceedings of the Association of American Geographers* 2 (1970): 145–49.

Index

Italics indicate topic is treated in detail.

Akin, Wallace E.	THE NORTH CENTRAL UNITED STATES
*Alexander, Lewis M.	THE NORTHEASTERN UNITED STATES
Booth, Charles W.	THE NORTHWESTERN UNITED STATES
Bradford, Sax	SPAIN IN THE WORLD
Cutshall, Alden	THE PHILIPPINES: Nation of Islands
Durrenberger, Robert	CALIFORNIA: The Last Frontier
*East, W. Gordon	THE SOVIET UNION
Goodwin, Harold L.	SPACE: Frontier Unlimited
Hansen, Niles M.	FRANCE IN THE MODERN WORLD
*Hall, Robert B., Jr.	JAPAN: Industrial Power of Asia
*Harrison Church, R. J.	WEST AFRICA: Environment and Policies
*Hart, John Fraser	THE SOUTH
Hodgson, Robert D. and Elvyn A. Stoneman	THE CHANGING MAP OF AFRICA, Second Edition
Hsieh, Chiao-min	CHINA: Ageless Land and Countless People
Jackson, W. A. Douglas	THE RUSSO-CHINESE BORDER LANDS: Zones of Peaceful Contact or Potential Conflicts? Second Edition
Karan, P. P. and William M. Jenkins, Jr.	THE HIMALAYAN KINGDOMS: Bhutan, Sikkim, and Nepal
Kish, George	ITALY
Mellor, Roy E. H.	COMECON: Challenge to the West
Momsen, Richard P., Jr.	BRAZIL: A Giant Stirs
Morris, John	THE SOUTHWESTERN UNITED STATES
Mulvihill, Donald F. and Ruth C. Mulvihill	GEOGRAPHY, MARKETING, AND URBAN GROWTH
*Neale, Walter C. and John Adams	INDIA: Search for Unity, Democracy and Progress
Nicholson, Norman L.	CANADA IN THE AMERICAN COMMUNITY
Niddrie, David L.	SOUTH AFRICA: Nation or Nations?
*Nystrom, J. Warren and George W. Hoffman	THE COMMON MARKET
Patton, Donald J.	THE UNITED STATES AND WORLD RESOURCES
*Petrov, Victor P.	CHINA: Emerging World Power
Pounds, Norman J. G.	DIVIDED GERMANY AND BERLIN
Ramazani, Rouhollah K.	THE NORTHERN TIER: Afghanistan, Iran, and Turkey
Stewart, Harris B., Jr.	THE GLOBAL SEA
Wiens, Herold J.	PACIFIC ISLAND BASTIONS OF THE UNITED STATES

* These titles are available in a second edition as of 1976.